LIFE™ BETWEEN PANELS

LIFE BETWEEN™ PANELS

THE COMPLETE TAILS OMNIBUS

ETHAN YOUNG

PRESIDENT & PUBLISHER **MIKE RICHARDSON**

EDITORS **SPENCER CUSHING & KEVIN BURKHALTER**

DESIGNER **ETHAN KIMBERLING**

DIGITAL ART TECHNICIAN **CHRISTINA McKENZIE**

SPECIAL THANKS: **For Shugie, the best studio-mate anyone could ask for.**

DarkHorse.com

First edition: April 2018
ISBN 978-1-50670-474-6

1 3 5 7 9 10 8 6 4 2
Printed in China

Published by Dark Horse Books
A division of Dark Horse Comics, Inc.
10956 SE Main Street
Milwaukie, OR 97222

Library of Congress Cataloging-in-Publication Data

Names: Young, Ethan, 1983- author, illustrator.
Title: Life between panels : the complete tails omnibus / Ethan Young.
Description: First edition. | Milwaukie, OR : Dark Horse Books, April 2018.
Identifiers: LCCN 2017049267 | ISBN 9781506704746 (paperback)
Subjects: LCSH: Graphic novels. | BISAC: COMICS & GRAPHIC NOVELS / General. | COMICS & GRAPHIC NOVELS / Nonfiction.
Classification: LCC PN6727.Y677 L54 2018 | DDC 741.5/973--dc23
LC record available at https://lccn.loc.gov/2017049267

FOREWORD

Best advice I can give to aspiring creators: finish your first project.

I dropped out of art school in 2002, eager to start my career. I initially dabbled with several pitches (including what is now *Nanjing: The Burning City*), but the bulk of 2002–2003 was spent developing a teen superhero book. I completed the first issue, then immediately redid the issue to make it better. Then I redid it again.

Being a perfectionist, I would neurotically stress over every panel, every line. I would redo page after page, because when you're young and untested, you fear two things: failure and criticism. I was proactively dodging both, but that's a fool's errand, as any pro will tell you. Perfection is an impossible standard you build for yourself. And here's the dirty little secret: *nobody cares except you.*

Enter fall of 2004. I had to get the monkey off my back and just focus on finishing something. I instituted a new rule for myself: no more revisions. The work didn't have to be perfect, it just had to be done. I committed all my energy to a new project that was simply groundbreaking: a semi-autobiographical comic about a struggling cartoonist. (Hold for applause.) It featured my then-girlfriend and a horde of fifteen cats. And that's how *Tails* was born.

I was 21 when this all went down, and completely unprepared for the daunting task of creating a three-issue mini-series. What resulted was crude, sloppy, and undisciplined. But according to some blogs, the comic also showed lots of promise. More importantly, I was no longer *Ethan Young, Aspiring Cartoonist.* I became *Ethan Young, Self Published Cartoonist With Newly Accrued Credit Card Debt.*

Fast forward to 2009. With the series drifting in creative limbo, I rebooted *Tails* as a webcomic, having redone nearly all of the original content. I broke my one new rule, but let's face it, I always knew I would. I was still chasing that elusive idea of perfection.

The webcomic garnered both praise and a much wider audience. (Thank you, internet!) I grounded the story deeper into my real life, even if I still leaned heavily on artistic license. I made my mother a supporting cast member, and introduced magical realism to spice up later chapters. I also made my cartoon facsimile look more Asian over time, as my work started to stray away from dominant western influences.

Through many ups and downs, I saw it through to the end. In early 2013, I inked the final page of *Tails.* It's a straightforward shot of our main protagonist chilling with his cats. Compare it to the opening page, and it almost looks like a different artist was in charge. (Which is a good thing.)

And that brings us to this handsome omnibus you have in your hands, *Life Between Panels*, a book that represents nearly a decade of work. Everything turned out all right for the struggling cartoonist who once fostered fifteen cats. He became a semi-successful cartoonist with a wife and son, and is now down to four cats.

While collecting this volume, I fought some pretty strong urges to revise any of the art. I wisely left the book as is. Because even though this comic was made to be shared, it's also my personal time capsule, offering me countless memories with just a quick glance. Seeing a specific page can remind me what I had on the TV for background noise, or how exhausted I was feeling.

So for all you aspiring creators, finish your first project. I promise you it'll be worth it. For all its narrative flaws and aesthetic inconsistencies, *Life Between Panels* captures me better than any other book I've worked on.

It'll never be perfect, but it's kinda perfect that way.

Ethan Young
2017

Here's one thing I've learned while living in New York City my entire life: rich, spoiled prunes can't WAIT to slap on their furs, even at the faintest sign of a chilly week.
CURL
VEGETARIAN LU
Oh, isn't that sweet? She's walking a LIVE dog to match the 40 SKINNED ones on her back (Yeah, yeah, consumer freedom and all that crap).
SIT, JUDY!

I SAID, 'SIT'!
Hey, wanna see something funny?
Oh, god...
Please don't...
HEY, LADY!
YOU LOOK LIKE A BEAR'S VAGINA!

HOW DARE YOU
SIN!
Oh, come on, Ethan! Don't you think it's time you grew some BALLS already?
They say that a keen observation is only called 'cynicism' by those who LACK it.
I can't remember who said that.
-sigh-

Okay, let's get the embarrassing stuff out of the way first: I'm a grown man still living with his parents. That's right--you HEARD me! (Don't judge me just yet, alright?) We're located in the Upper East Side--a flawless, picture-perfect neighborhood. (You can't tell, but I just rolled my eyes...)
Hey, look, there's my building. It doesn't have the same charm as those antique-y brownstones, but it's still pretty fancy.
Whenever my friends see my place, they just assume that I must be livin' it up like a KING...

You can call her Sin (It's not her real name), and I'm Ethan (Just in case you didn't catch that earlier).

I've got two jobs: animal caretaker and cartoonist. Though lately, cartooning has become more like a hobby--but isn't that always the case when artists get day jobs? Oh, if you're wondering about this couch...

My room has essentially been transformed into a CAT HOUSE -- a place for rescued strays and unwanted pets.
TOBEY
CLARKIE
BRAM
LIL' BUB
LANA
CHEWIE & HONEY
MURDOCK
OTHELLO
PETEY
Then there's my bathroom. For the past three months or so (I lose count), I've been fostering these four kittens for the local animal shelter (my humble place of work).
Oh, and wait, before I forget -- this here is Shugie. She's the little runt. (The other cats in my bedroom would tear her apart.)
SNIFF SNIFF
Hey, Sweetie.

By the way, today's a special day. Some space has freed up at the shelter-- so the kittens are FINALLY leaving my BATHROOM!
Come on. I wanted to get going before my dad woke up.
-GRUNT-
-GRUNT-
TOO LATE...
CLEAN UP CAT SHIT!
Nothing wakes you up like the sight of SAGGY MAN-BOOBS.

Litter box maintenance takes more or less half an hour out of my daily morning ritual. I'd get it done MUCH faster if the cats didn't insist on engulfing me while I worked. Let's face it -- they have no real concept of what I'm doing. And NO-- it's NOT as cute as it looks!
Guys... I'll feed you after I'm done...
BIG STINKY!
OH... THE HUMANITY...
The kittens are an entirely different monster. Do not be fooled by their cuteness. They've yet to learn how to distinguish their litter boxes from ANYTHING ELSE THEY CAN TOUCH. That makes them the DEVIL.
Did I mention that they're LEAVING?

So, when will I finally get to see those new pages that you're submitting? Your MAGNUM OPUS...
Not yet. I don't really... wanna jinx it, you know?
Come on -- just finish eating so we can go, all right? I'm already running late.
Jeez... you want me to pull that stick out of your butt first?

Did you eat breakfast yet? Just let me make some eggs for you.
Mom--you know I'm vegan. Give up already...
I'm here to take care of you, son.
Meet my mom--the most essential human being in my life. She was diagnosed with Multiple Sclerosis over a decade ago (hence the cane). I try and help out around the house as much as I can, but she's fairly self-sufficient, all things considered.
Your... Your brother called last night. I told him you were out...
You should call him, son--talk to him. He misses you...
I'm already late, Mom. Gotta run,
MUAH
Okay...

So spill it, Ethan, why so distant? Harboring some state secret?
I'm fine--REALLY. You don't have to tag along today. I can bring these little buggers in myself.
Yeah, but it'd be nice to see the peeps again.
Who WILLINGLY wants to work during their break?
Lemme tell you... ANYTHING beats class right now. I'd much rather be cleaning cages than sitting through one of Mr. Roe's lectures.

Mr. Roe. Wasn't that the guy you wanted to drop? He's that guy who's, like, a massive dick, right?
Yeah, BIG TIME. But unfortunately, I need his class for PRE-MED. Whatcha gonna do, right?
Well... okay, then. Just wanna make sure you're happy with school and everything.
Don't worry so much about me. "I'M FINE, REALLY."
Sin and I have been together since high school. She was my first REAL girlfriend ('REAL' meaning we did more than just hold hands).
What was that? An impression of me?

In fact, Sin is the whole reason for this little CAT CRUSADE of mine. Seriously, I didn't even LIKE cats before we started dating. Anyhoo...
2575
...Sin left for school last year and we're doing (or at least TRYING to do) this long-distance thing. I'm still adjusting -- which is hard when you have eleven cats.
EXIT
NEWSSTAN
God bless...

This is where I spend about forty hours of my week: The Humane Society of Manhattan. Besides being an animal shelter, this place also has a low-cost clinic.
HUMANE SOCIETY of MANHATTAN
24 EAST 16
ANIMAL HOSPITAL
We get our fair share of idiots and wackos.
SHE'S OBESE?!
I swear, Doc-- this tumor just came out of NOWHERE!
HMM... I'm not very fond of the claws. Can I have them removed?
WHY SHOULD I HAVE TO PAY?! YOU'RE THE ONE WHO DISCOVERED THE PROBLEM!

Ah, the beginning of another beautiful day...

ETHAN! Do you have ANY idea what time it is?
Sorry, April! Here--blame the kittens--or SIN.
HEY.
Listen up! Martha needs to see you.
THE DREADFUL BOSS...
ETHAN, why did you get here so late today?! April had to give breakfast to all the cats in your ward--AND she walked all the dogs by herself.
I get here ALL the way from JERSEY! I always manage to get here on time!
Yeah, like I give ashit.
Do it for the animals, okay?
I know that, Martha...
You damn GOBLIN...

ETHAN...
YOU FOOL...
YOU'LL BE MY LITTLE BITCH FOR ALL ETERNITY!
Don't make me angry, BANANA-BOOBS!
You wouldn't like me when I'm angry...
ETHAN!

Get back to work...

RING TONE
Hey--get that for me! I'm tryin' to pill Leo here.
Aw, poor Leo...
It's Patrick... Should I pick up?
No.
You sure now?
JUST FUCK HIM.
Ugh... goddamnit...
HEY, I NEED SOME HELP WITH LEO HERE! I'M NOT GONNA LOSE AN EYE OVER THIS!

You know, Hemingway had a lot of cats too. Ethan's just stressed, that's all. You know how this place can get.
Yeah, I know...
Plus--he's got his whole ART thing. His new stuff took a lot out of him.
WAIT--when did you see his new artwork?
Around last week.

You constipated or something?

Funny...

Ethan... is this about that stupid argument you had with your brother last week?

It wasn't THAT stupid...

I don't even know why you let him get to you...

Can't you just TUNE him out?

Patrick is over thirty and he's SINGLE and he's really WEIRD. What the hell does HE know about fostering KITTENS? Who's HE to talk?

It's not that, really. Pat's been giving me shit since I quit art school. It's nothing new.

Then?
God, this isn't... this isn't how I imagined my life, that's all...
It isn't...
I thought... by the time I was twenty-two, I'd be a world-famous comic artist.
I'd have my own place--
--and it wouldn't matter HOW MANY strays we wanted to rescue, you know?
Yeah...
-sigh-
This place was only meant to be a part-time job.
Now it's my entire life.
Hey... at least you're in good company.
Hemingway was an OLD CAT LADY, too.
The man shot himself, didn't he?

Hey, kids.
I know--
the cage
life sucks.
It does...
But I guarantee
you'll find a
nice home
to scratch
up soon...
-MEOW-
-MEOW-
-MEOW-
You'll find
a MUCH better
home than
my bathroom--
that's for sure.
I'll see you
kids later...

Canarsie, Brooklyn

So, did you get your first report card yet?
Dad, I don't think that anyone refers to them as 'report cards' when you're going to college.
Well, the most important thing is to keep your grades up-- don't forget that...
Yeah...

...listen, Penelope, until you've worked at a shelter, you have no idea how stressful it can get--leave Ethan alone.
WHAT? (GOD, you're so horrible sometimes...)
...say that again? Nope, haven't mentioned it to my dad...
Yes, yes, I know-- I have to tell him one of these days...

KLIK
Coast is clear...
CLEAN UP CAT SHIT!!

Will our daring CRUSADER CAT escape the evil clutches of the MENACING POOCH?!
CAT ST
ONE WAY

Can he THWART the SINISTER SQUIRREL?!

Of course he can! He's CRUSADER CAT! Bold defender of CATROPOLIS!
Ever noble and brave--with a sharp wit to boot! PLUS--look at how ADORABLE he is!
Okay, Tobey... I get it. I'm not exactly a POET.
I'll stop torturing you for now.
HEY, YOU HAVE MAIL!
God, why is he STILL yelling?
CHEWIE!! I JUST cleaned that! COME ON!

RING TONE
Hey.
...no, I was just washing up a bit. What's up?
OH.
...I'm sorry to hear that, baby. That's--
--look, I know you're upset--
--Ethan, could you calm down, please?

I AM CALM.
I'M JUST PISSED OFF! This was only my back-up company, too! They publish CRAP comics! And they had the NERVE to tell me that I need to `improve my craft'. Yeah, I'll improve my foot up their ass!
GOD!!
Then why should it matter so much, Ethan? Since they're crap...
Ugh--PLEASE, Cynthia--don't do the whole `DEVIL'S ADVOCATE' thing. I'm in no FUCKIN' MOOD...
I WASN'T--forget it, Ethan. We're back to where we were FIVE hours ago! You should be MEDICATED!
GEE, THANKS! YOU'RE SUCH AN ANGEL! WHAT GREAT FUCKIN' SUPPORT!
ESPECIALLY SINCE I'M TAKING CARE OF ALL THE DAMN CATS BY MYSELF HERE!

Ethan -- I'm also stressed, alright?! Do you think school is PLAYTIME?
OH, COME ON! We both know you're not gonna stick with PRE-MED anyway!
WHAT -- you want me to quit school and stay here to take care of all this SHIT with you?! You're such an ASSHOLE!
CYNTHIA... JUST GO FUCK YOURSELF, OKAY?!
GO FUCK YOURSELF AND DON'T TALK TO ME!
THAT WORK FOR YOU?!!
CLICK
WHY YOU YELL?! STOP YELLING

God bless, sir...
Babe--why on GOD'S GREEN EARTH did you give that guy a bill?
It's cold--give the poor guy a damn break.
He's just gonna buy CRACK with it. COME ON!
Contrary to popular belief, sweetheart--
--not every homeless person is addicted to crack.
OH, BLAH!

You ever heard of redemption?
Come here, little buddy...
LIMP LIMP

PLEASE
HELP
$

ETHAN-- I can't BELIEVE you said that to her! Don't you know ANYTHING about women?
OKAY, OKAY-- don't rub it in...
FATTY
I was frustrated-- taking care of all the cats by myself. I just... this isn't the IDEAL situation, you know?
Yeah, it's called LIFE, Ethan. Are you and Cynthia at least on speaking terms?
Nope. It was a pretty BIG fight.
I'm sure that things will work out for the best.
I guess...

April... be honest with me. Brutally honest.
On a scale from one to ten, how much of an ASS was I?
On a scale from one to ten? Not great. But look, nobody's perfect. I've seen and HAD worse boyfriends than you. Don't beat yourself up.
But if I HAD to score you... then I'd give you a seven.
Huh... that's better than I expected.
Now-- don't forget. You have to thoroughly soak the dog food before feeding it to the pigeon. That bird needs the extra protein.
I find it TERRIBLY disturbing that this is CHICKEN flavored.
?
DRY FOO

Mount Holyoke University
South Hadley, Massachusetts
How long ago did they break up?
Probably during the break, maybe? I'm not really sure.
KEEP OUT
Cynthia? It's Penelope and Liz. Come on--get dressed and we'll all grab some food...

SIN?

Try and call Cynthia again, son...

Mom, I tried texting her last week -- no response. If she wants to call, she will call.
Well, it would make me VERY happy. You don't want your mom to be SAD, do you?
I thought you never even LIKED Cynthia.
Nonsense! I was just concerned when you started dating. You were both so young...
Well -- three years went by and we didn't need a single abortion...
Don't speak that way...
Sorry...

What about the cats, son? They're HER responsibility too. Why do you like those cats so much?
Because they don't ask a million questions. Can we talk about something else, Mom?
Have you called Patrick lately?
-sigh-
You two used to be so close. I remember when the two of you would spend the entire summer just drawing and drawing.
Mom, that's because you wouldn't let us out of the apartment.
Well, look at where we used to live. Remember all the gangsters that would hang around Chinatown?
You should be thanking me, son! I kept you boys safe-- I kept you from being mugged.
HURRAY! We kept our food stamps safe!

You're so lucky you don't have to deal with women, little buddy...
LOOK! BIRD DROPPINGS!
WHOA.
It looks like you're almost ready to go back out there...
Almost...

Every fuckin' day is the same, kid! EVERY DAMN DAY! Sooner or later, it's gonna get to you. Just wait and see!
You come in, wash your hands, and you MUTILATE all these furry nutsacks!
Dogs, cats, even gerbils! I've touched a gerbil's BALLS, son! You got any idea what those feel like? HUH?! Goddamnit, get the hell outta here while you STILL CAN!!
In case you're wondering, the question was, "How's your day been, Doc?"
Oh, god... the blood, son, the blood...
MOVE, ELEVATOR, MOVE!!
April and I escaped work early that day to hang out with her friend, Ash, who was in town. After a few beers, the conversation somehow landed on my cats...

Long story short -- my ex had a cat in her back yard who popped out a LOT of babies. I took in a litter of four (Murdack, Tobey, Chewie and Honey) while Sin took in a litter of five (Lana, Clarkie, Lil'Bub, Bram and Petey). Then there's the older sibling, Shugie, who's a little runt. So, when Sin left for Massachusetts, her litter came to live with mine. Oh, and there's also Othello, who's the only cat that's not related -- he came from an old classmate who didn't want him anymore.

Um... yeah... so, that's basically how I ended up with ELEVEN CATS...

Wow... you're an old cat lady.

Oh, he knows it.

Wait...

Did I mention the bird?

So, did you ever text Ethan back?
I really wanted to, but I chickened out. We'd just end up yelling anyway...
Then... you haven't actually spoken to Ethan for--
For, like, about SIX weeks now... maybe even more. Ethan and I are both trying to avoid the ELEPHANT in the room.
I mean, Ethan doesn't even speak to his own BROTHER now-- all over some dumb argument a while back concerning the cats.
Well, if that were the case, I'd imagine that Ethan had issues with his brother prior to that one argument.

Oh, yeah, totally. But in Ethan's defense, I'm sure he was just defending himself, you know?
mmhmm...
And I can relate, 'cause my family thinks I'm weird, too. I mean, the only reason Ethan is taking care of MY cats right now is 'cause I knew that my dad wouldn't. See... at times, Ethan can be super-sweet like that. Then OTHER times-- he's a total DICKMOUTH.
Speaking of your father, have you talked to him yet? About taking some time off from school?
See, to my dad, that would just come across as QUITTING. There's no way he'd understand. I mean, I don't want to sound ungrateful. I know that I'm lucky to be in such a good school--but I'm only in PRE-MED 'cause of my dad. I hate science...
-SIGH- Why do all men SUCK, Deena?
Wish I could tell you...

You know-- we can always hire a hitman to neuter him.
Don't be a bitch, Penelope.

I mean, I've got NO idea how we'd go about hiring somebody like that -- but how hard can it REALLY be, you know?
OOH--HEY! Maybe we could get a souvenir too! Do you want some nu--
7pm
PENELOPE -- I appreciate the support--but I don't wanna be the VINDICTIVE EX FROM HELL.
Really?

Have you forgotten all the CRAP times with Ethan?
That'd be impossible...
Hey, you two.
What's up?
Hey, Julia.
Penelope-- I'll be fine, okay?
Whatever... I just need to get you drunk.

There's a party at the DELLES tonight and--
HOLD UP-- I got a text.
♪RING TONE♪
Don't even THINK about it...
People just assume that working with cute, fuzzy animals is some kind of wonderful dream...

... but working with animals in shelters is a whole other story. Most of these guys spend so much of their day stuck in cages -- they've lost what made them animals in the first place.
Take Gavin here for example. He's been at the Humane Society for almost half a year now.
I'M TELLIN' YOU!
GAVIN IS INSANE!
CRAIG
Last Friday, Gavin 'attacked' several of my coworkers. One in particular believes that Gavin is slowly becoming mentally unstable.

How does ANYONE stay sane around here? Even though we're in an animal shelter-- we're never short on human drama.
WHAT?! YOU CAN'T TAKE HIM?!
LOOK, SIR-- there's simply no space left-- not a single cage, okay?
SORRY-- you'll have to take him to another shelter.
-WHIMPER-

Thanks for NOTHING, lady...

At least there's SOME good news. Remember that litter I fostered? Well, the last remaining critter is finally getting adopted today. They named her Cher (God, I know), and she's all grown up now. With so many animals in need of homes -- I consider this to be a tiny miracle.
So, how about it, Ethan? Party in Bushwick tonight?
I know it'll interfere with your usual night of sulking and masturbation--but there's gonna be booze and girls. Those things go hand in hand!
HMMM?
You're a bloody traitor to your own gender--you know that, April?
Ethan--glad you're here! I want you to meet Cher's new MOMMY...

And so, the INCREDIBLE ETHAN found himself face to face with his old, ugly nemesis... THE FEROCIOUS FUR LADY !!
You'll be no match for me this time --I'm wearing a whole family of POLAR BEARS! Even your feline friend can't save you now!
Pleased to meet you...

WHAT THE FUCK?
Yeah... and that's pretty much how I got fired. Neat, huh?
Martha dragged me up to her office and thoroughly explained the meaning of the word 'RUDE' to me.
This coming from a lady who wants to give our animals to someone who thinks of them as accessories.
Technically speaking -- I was 'let go'.
And here I thought the day was looking up.

PRE MIDTERM DASH
Sin?
SIN?
Jesus, where the heck is that girl?
Penelope... Hey, sexypants...
Ah, fuck...

Good LORD, Sin!
...come gimme a kiss now, baby...
...you know you want it...
So I did end up going to that party in Bushwick--mainly to score some free alcohol...
I figured that since I lost my job-- I might as well try and drink my worries away. (FYI, that's only my THIRD beer.) This sure as hell beats sitting at home tonight.
Also, getting tipsy DOES have a plus side to it...

I was actually capable of meeting new people...
SHE stood out immediately. I love the cute, nerdy types...
BURP!
Her name's Sally, by the way...

Something wrong? You've been quiet all night.
No, um, nothing, Sally...
Come on, Ethan, admit it...
You miss me...
And you still want me...

Sin, I...
You know that I can satisfy you FAR BETTER than little Miss White Bread here...

Sorry, I've lost the mood...

ONE MONTH LATER!

Um, hello. Hi. SUPER EGO MAGAZINE?

Hi, hi. I'm trying to get in contact with your art editor, if possible.

I sent over a copy of my portfolio about --
(LANA, STOP THAT!)
-- about three weeks ago. I'm just --

Oh, okay, I see. Thanks anyway. (FUCKERS!)

LOOK! My leg is not a piece of WOOD, okay?!

It's been six weeks since I've drawn anything. (Or was it seven?) SIX. Yeah, it's SIX.
Can I just call it a FUNK? I won't feel as guilty that way.
Now I've sunk so low as to pity myself. Wonderful.

I talked with Mom --but her advice is always less than helpful.

Son, you can go back to school. Become a doctor--or lawyer! You'll need a secure job to support your family.

But THANK THE HEAVENS I've got Dad here.

NO MARRY THAT WHITE GIRL! YOU GO GET GOOD CHINESE WIFE! MAKE CHINESE BABIES!!

And last night, with Sally, I accidentally called her 'SIN.' (YIKES!) I tried to play it off...

I told her that it was my new 'naughty nickname' for her. Ha... Do you ever miss Cynthia?

Goodnight, Shugie.

Sweet dreams.

Hey, who wants bird seed?
You think you're ready, little guy?
CLEAN UP--
YES, I KNOW!
(YOU BARBARIAN.)

Fuckin' droppings...
Son--
Your brother is going to come home for lunch tomorrow afternoon. I'll prepare a dish without meat for you...
ECO
Mom, you already know what I'll say...
Oh, but it's been so long since--
MOM!
CRAP. Why did I have to do that?
-sigh- I need some more soap. Excuse me, Mom...

Ms. Lee--
your grades have been steadily declining.
I'd recommend some tutoring.
Your father is a dear friend and colleague of mine, so I would hate to see you fail...

Dad, no, it's -- it's not like I'm tryin' to waste your money. But I'm not -- what? DAD, quit mentioning that -- I don't drink on a nightly basis! That was a PARTY!
Mr. Reynolds is just exaggerating -- don't take his word so seriously. That last test was--
-sigh- You're not even listening to me, Dad...
Ugh... well, I might as well cough it up now...

I finally got my father on the phone--told him I wanna drop out.
Did he disown you?
No, just a mild stroke...
YO! WHAT THE HELL?!
sniff sniff
You DONE?!
Court order, Sin.

Penelope
I went to New York. Don't hate me. Wish me luck instead. xo, Sin
Ah, shit...
So--how are things going with Sally? Still having mediocre, mechanical sex?

Ethan... I don't think we should see each other anymore. It's not working out...
You're a bit of a downer, Ethan. Come on--you don't even have a JOB right now. ALSO--and this is not against YOU--but I was a tad freaked out with all that 'naughty nickname' talk. I'm not into DIRTY stuff.
Actually, we broke up. She dumped me while we were having lunch yesterday.
WHOOPS. Great, now I feel like a DICK. Please tell me she paid for her own meal...

Hey, sorry for springing this on you, Ethan. But... are you still planning to pick up the check?
PUT FORK DOWN...
SURE...
Look at it this way-- you weren't even all that crazy about her.
I'll be the first to admit-- it was a BORING relationship. But...it's... it wasn't BAD. Nobody wants to die alone -- so cut me some damn slack, okay?
You're too young to be dwelling on your death. Calm down. With THAT kind of mentality, you'll just end up crawling back to her.
Care to make it interesting $?

SALLY! PLEASE, PLEASE GIVE ME ANOTHER CHANCE! I KNOW THAT I CAN BECOME THE KIND OF MAN YOU WANT!
I SWEAR, SALLY! I CAN CHANGE! I REALLY THINK WE'VE GOT SOMETHING SPECIAL HERE!

This is not the time, Ethan...
NYU

Hey, I'm Alex...

FUCK YOU!! ARE YOU DUMPING ME FOR THIS DICK WITH A JEWFRO?!

Great... now I'm out twenty BUCKS...

I need to HIT something. ANYTHING...
Even that PARKING METER would do...
Hey, STUD! I'm FUCKING your EX, which makes you LESS OF A MAN!
FUCK...
FUCK!
FUCK!
FUCK!
Dude, some guy's doing KUNG FU out here!

In case you're wondering...
The 'B' stands for, "Boy, your EX sure loves havin' SEX with me!" And I can also grow facial hair. Compare yourself to me and then WEEP, you little man!
I got the rubber! Let's DO it in front of him!
You read my mind, baby!
HA HA HA HA HA HA HA HA HA HA HA
Man, being homeless ain't as bad as being THAT guy!
HA HA HA HA HA
HA HA HA HA HA HA HA HA HA

Our emasculated hero rampages through the streets of New York, leaving a path of utter destruction. He will have his revenge on CAPTAIN JEWFRO!
Ethan...
Hey, I was just coming from Mom's.
What's up?
Why, hello, Patrick...

FIVE MINUTES LATER...
All right, my new pet peeve: BEING PUNCHED IN THE FACE.
GOD...
And NO--this is NOT my fault. Pat was being MR. FUCKIN' KNOW-IT-ALL!
Look-- Mom told me about your job situation...
Seriously-- if there's any way I can help...
Man--what an arrogant asshole...
Finally -- I let him have it.
PATRICK! STAY OUT OF MY LIFE AND JUST GO FUCK YOURSELF!
And guess what? He even started to CRY!
HA! LOSER!

Finally remembered that old saying...

"The power of accurate observation is commonly called cynicism by those who have not got it." It was George Bernard Shaw who said that. Nobel Prize, my ass--

"Hey, you..."

Oh, shit...
are you
okay?

No...
Not
really...

Okay, so here's the story so far...
Our hero, Crusader Cat, has just been ambushed! He gets hit by this BIG ENERGY BLAST! BOOM!!! He looks up and guess who he sees...
Sit down, my fearsome feline! RELAX! You're not going anywhere--not while you're at the whim of RATSO BLASTO!

WHAT ON EARTH DID YOU HIT ME WITH, **YOU STUPID JERK?!!**

OH, SOMETHING YOU'VE DESERVED FOR A VERY LONG TIME! I'VE USED MY **SUCKO RAY** TO SUCK YOU DRY...

OF ALL YOUR POWERS, THAT IS!

So now--you think Ratso Blasto has got Crusader all cornered--powerless to even put up a fight! But then, suddenly--

HEY, UGLY!!

THE MASKED HOUND & RABBIT X!

HA!! AWESOME, ISN'T IT?!

Well, trust me, Shugie--
it's pretty awesome.

DING DONG
Uh oh... you better hide, baby...
Heya, Boris...
What can I help you with?
A lot of food for just the two cats.
Well, they're BIG eaters, these two...
Othello
Tobey
I WATCH YOU, BOY...

You see, besides Tobey and Othello here--
--the rest of my cats are total wimps, which means they're great at hiding...
SHUGIE
HONEY
CHEWIE
MURDOCK
Welcome to my new home in Williamsburg, Brooklyn. At last, a little freedom from my folks. I moved in with April about three months ago, after one of her roommates completely bailed out on her without so much as a notice.

STRANGE, isn't it? Last time you saw me, I looked like a CYCLOPS. Not to mention the fact that my EX (THE EX) had suddenly materialized out of nowhere. I'm sure you were all thinking the exact same thing-- that somehow, Sin and I were gonna reconcile and live happily ever after and make lotsa FAT babies, right? Well, tough shit.
Although Sin was making concrete plans to move back to NYC--she assured me that there was NO CHANCE IN HELL of us ever getting back together. "I just need closure," she said.
SEX
SEX SEX SEX SEX SEX SEX SEX SEX SEX SEX SEX SEX SEX SEX SEX SEX SEX SEX SEX SEX SEX SEX SEX SEX SEX SEX
Yeah, WHATEVER. She kept going on and ON about how immature and self-centered I was. (I dunno, I wasn't really paying attention to her stupidness...)
It was the final nail. I think I handled it fairly well...
WHY?!

The following weeks were... odd. Sin made several trips to pick up Lana, Bram, Petey, Lil' Bub, and Clarkie. The whole thing unfolded like some bizarre divorce settlement. Some couples separate the CHINA, others separate CATS.
I wasted a lot of time sulking in what USED to be my bedroom...
I was in a RUT. I needed some change--BIG CHANGE. I decided... I needed a good, fresh start.
Which meant moving out...
As much as I was gonna miss the other cats--NOT having them around made it a BILLION times easier to look for a new place. Most people don't even wanna live with ONE cat--let alone a DOZEN. But... as luck would have it--April's roommate fiasco was my blessing in disguise.
RULE #7: YOU PICK UP EVERY LAST PIECE OF CAT HAIR.

There's me, April, and Brian. Brian is a nudist--and quite proud of it, too. He and April have lived together for years now--so she's no longer phased by the sight of his pecker. Me--I'm still adjusting...
Don't get me wrong--Brian's a nice guy. And the cats take to him. He's like a cat himself: hairy and naked.
Oh, hey, Tobey!
I've got myself a pretty sweet setup here. My room's just big enough for my comics, an art table, my bed, a litter box. You know, all the essentials.
These days, I'm trying my best to earn a living with my art. Just random freelance jobs, nothing too exciting. It does, however, help to pay the rent and feed all the cats.
I'll let you all know when something interesting comes up...

The next morning, I wake up and find a LOVELY surprise from the kids. You might want to close your eyes.
-GASP-
A HAIRBALL! LOOK AT THE SIZE OF THAT THING! AND RIGHT ON THE CARPET, TOO!
RISE AND SHINE, SWEET CHEEKS!
YAWN...
Oh, terrific...
Morning?
Hello...

Quick question--have you even bothered to meet the other tenants yet?
Oh, hey, I'm Mark. You just move in?
Yeah, hey, howzit hangin'?
I moved out to get some privacy--not to start a book club, April...
Ethan, I just don't wanna see you transform into a hermit, okay? I've barely seen you hang out any later than, like, 7 p.m. or something.
Look--Ash is in town. We're gonna do food, drinks and FUN. Interested? This'll be GOOD for you, trust me.

I've hung out past seven before. MANY times, in fact!
Sure...
She's one of those post-college smartasses with no real ambition or career-- just a string of odd jobs.
I've noticed this a lot more since moving in here--April is insanely bossy and judgemental.
I know that sounds a tad cruel, but April knows it as well. She's a 'LIFE SUCKS' kinda gal...
You should maybe fix your hair a bit...
Ergo--she compensates by criticizing everyone and everyTHING around her.
Hey, wait a second! What's wrong with my hair?!
MORNING, GUYS!

All right, let me catch you up to speed. Last we saw of CRUSADER CAT, he was being rescued by the MASKED HOUND and RABBIT X. Now we see him waking up--still very, very disoriented. He notices this unfamiliar face...

Wh-- Who are you?

My name is Galen. Don't be startled...

Your friends brought you here after saving you from that mad rodent. You need rest...

Galen's this old, retired hero. His name has become urban legend. He was BADASS back in the day though--nicknamed the 'TECHNO TURTLE.' So, naturally, he's the most qualified to explain to Crusader--

The core of Ratso's Sucko Ray must be the KARZONIAN GEM--the only known object capable of neutralizing your powers. How he OBTAINED the GEM is the question at hand...

Crusader is devastated by this news, obviously. You know, he figured Ratso was just bluffing or something. And the thing is--Ratso is still on the loose...
We're sorry, Crusader. Here--want a bite of my carrot?
Hmph. Thanks for trying, kid...
You should stay here with Galen--try to see if these effects can be reversed. As for Ratso--leave him to us. You are no match for that fiend in your current condition...
He's right, I'm afraid. Fighting Ratso would be SUICIDE. You are a mere mortal now...
NO, GUYS! Ratso is still MY responsibility--powers or not!
Bring me whatever weapons I can use, Galen! Anything that I can LIFT!
I have a suit you could use--but are you SURE about this?

And so...
Sorry, I can't just SIT here while Ratso's out there harming innocent animals...
That's not what HEROES are made of!
"Ethan, as much as I'd love to hear the rest of this--"
--we're not gonna meet anyone if we're just gonna sit here.

ASH--we both know Ethan won't even TALK to a girl unless he's DRUNK--and he hasn't even taken a single SIP tonight.
...
Hey, hey, don't worry about it. I'll teach you my method--it can't fail.
METHOD? You mean being popular and Irish isn't enough?
Oh, how young and naive, my boy! Let me break it down for you. Everyone needs social proof--they need to be noticed, heard--they need people to tell them they're attractive. With the one and only ASH McCARRICK METHOD, you use that to your advantage. You have to DENY the other person social proof. Start by talking--nothing too heavy (maybe a flirtatious joke or two). AND THEN--
HUH? What was that? Sorry--I was distracted by something FAR more interesting.
So... your method is essentially about being a DICK...
Well, yes, if you want to go and be GLIB about it...

Look--don't listen to him. He's a DRUNK and a moron to boot. I'VE got the perfect girl for you, Ethan.
She's a new volunteer at the shelter. Cute, smart, loves cats and COMICS.
Want me to set up a little MEET & GREET? A search for Spark? Eh?
-clicks tongue-
You can turn off the 'sleazy matchmaker' talk, April. I just don't--
This is utterly pathetic. How can you stand this pity party?
Just tell them the TRUTH, Ethan. You're not ready to meet anyone because of ME. You've been thinking more and more about me--no matter how hard that cute little brain of yours tries to FIGHT it...

Nice outfit. You've got that whole 'Tricia Helfer' thing goin' on...
Oolala... breaking out the sarcasm already? You might have a SPINE after all. But don't worry--I didn't show up to argue all night. I'm only here, Ethan--
--TO SAY HI.
GAH!!
Whoa, Ethan! Careful!
Ethan... you scared us for a second there. You okay?

I... I know you still have feelings for me, Ethan. I understand that, really. I know that this will take some TIME for you...
But please understand that I just CAN'T be with you anymore. Okay? And... promise me you won't sit around and PINE over me.
That would just be pathetic.
Yeah, so's your FACE!
-sigh-
Shoulda said it when I had the CHANCE.
I haven't been able to sleep much since I saw Sin at that bar. (Ugh... wait, did I just say 'SAW'? Okay, I really AM going INSANE.)
YAWN
YAWN

Since roommate bonding was required with Brian, I figured I'd talk to him about it. Seriously, I needed to talk to someone (besides April for once), and Brian was a third-year Psych Major. If anyone could help me figure this out, he was the guy...
...and you actually saw her as a MONSTER?
Um... not exactly, no...
It's kinda hard to pin down. Basically, I've been 'seeing' Sin, envisioning her. It's been on and off for the past several months. Sometimes I'm just daydreaming, while other times it feels more like a hallucination.
But the other night -- it felt different. It was creepy. It felt all too real -- even when she went all 'Harvey Dent' on me. I wasn't drunk or anything, by the way. The whole situation was just... eerie. Any thoughts, man?
Well, PARANOID SCHIZOPHRENIA immediately comes to mind...
HAR HAR HAR
You're just externalizing your loss in order to cope with it, man. Don't let it ruin you.

Anyway, it's late. Gonna hit the hay. I suggest you do the same, dude. Get some zzz's.
MMM-HMM. Thanks, Brian...
As I sat there drinking solo, I came to realize two things. 1.) Brian's lovers must be VERY satisfied. And 2.) Maybe my problem is... I've been focusing way too much attention on my EX-- and not nearly enough on MYSELF. Sounds a bit selfish, I know. But still...
I have my own personal life. And I have my friends. And I have my WORK.
Why was I wasting so much effort creating elaborate fantasies revolving around HER?
THAT DOES IT! As soon as I'm done with this lager here, I'm gonna march STRAIGHT into my room and DRAW! I've got my CAREER to think about, goddamnit!
(And there's nothing like WORK to keep your mind off women.)

Like I said earlier-- freelancing rarely offers up anything that's interesting and/or cool.
Nevertheless, last Thursday, I landed myself an extremely... UNIQUE gig (to say the least).
GAY PORN. That's right, you heard me...
It's a natural fit when you think about it-- it's just like drawing SUPER HEROES...
Except without the clothes...
And there are LOTS of them...

Not bad--if I do say so myself. Of course, we'll have to wait and see what the client thinks.
TOO STRAIGHT? Did I just hear you right, Grant?
Yes, Ethan, it looks too STRAIGHT-- as in too HETERO! I don't see ANY passion on the page here. This is supposed to be EROTICA, Ethan. But all I see right now: topless straight dudes hugging each other.
Half of them aren't even LOOKING at each other. Is this how you think gay men have sex?
Just fix it for me, okay? Thanks.

So what have you been drawing lately, son? You seem so busy--I hardly get to see you now...
Sorry, MOM, I know. But hey, being busy is GOOD. I even have a meeting with a comic editor later this week. He's interested in hearing about Crusader Cat.
Oh, that's WONDERFUL news. You should let your brother know about it...
Mom, the last time I bumped into Patrick, it didn't end on good terms.
Let's leave it at that.
Don't you see why that makes me sad? You're FAMILY. You'll know one day when you have kids of your own.
HA. KIDS?
Trust me, son, you'll be thinking about kids soon--you're at that age. But you need to find the right person soon--before you get too old.
MOM--I'm just DATING for now--not looking for my soulmate. Got a date tonight, in fact.
Oh...is she... CHINESE?

Due to EXTREME peer pressure -- I agreed to let April set me up on a blind date. Since the weather has been so kind to us lately, we all decided to have dinner on the roof. Makes the night extra special. Heck, Brian even got dressed --
--in a manner of speaking.
That's, uh, quite the bathrobe there, Brian. Looking both SEXY AND comfortable.
Well, I gotta try my best. I don't look HALF as good as YOU tonight, though.
HEY, EVERYONE! WE'RE HERE! AND WE GOT THE BOOZE!
HEY, HEY--REMEMBER-- USE THE METHOD, ETHAN. METHOD ALL THE WAY. TRUST ME, IT NEVER FAILS.
QUIET.
Hi, um, glad you could make it. I'm April's roommate, Ethan. How are you?

Um... we've met...
Hey... waitaminute...
Five minutes later...
You tried to set me up with somebody who HATES me, April! Jesus CHRIST! Didn't you bother to find out that she's SIN'S FRIEND?!
Ethan, Ethan, I'm sorry. In hindsight, I probably shoulda done a more extensive background check.
Um... Ash is hitting on her...
-sigh-

Okay, now we're getting to the REAL action. Picture this: Ratso has unleashed a reign of TERROR all across the streets of CATROPOLIS! Nobody is powerful enough to stop him. We finally begin to see Ratso for what he truly is: ONE EVIL BASTARD.
Y--YOU'LL NEVER GET AWAY WITH THIS, RATSO!
YOU INSOLENT FOOL! THERE ARE NO CATS IN TIGHTS TO SAVE THE DAY!
THINK AGAIN, BUCK-TOOTH!!

FFOOMMM
WHOOSH! Crusader comes soaring in with a vengeance! He's got his new POWER SUIT and he's ready to give Ratso a good old-fashioned beatdown!
We're gonna lock you away and throw away the key, Ratso! Now SPILL it! How did you get the KARZONIAN GEM?!!
Heh... you're d-dumber than you look, Crusader...
Keep in mind, Ratso may be evil, but he's no genius. There had to be somebody engineering his plans...
Finally, Crusader comes face to face with the evil puppetmaster.

GALEN! -GASP- THE SINISTER MASTERMIND!!
This shocking betrayal is simply...well...SHOCKING!
"Well, Ethan, I've gotta say--"
--THIS IS GREAT! Perfect for our kids' line at LOCUSTS COMICS!
WOW, REALLY? I mean--ahem--really? 'Cause that'd be neat...

Oh, definitely! The other editors are gonna love this, I'm sure of it. I do have ONE suggestion-- a MINOR one...
Sure, shoot.
Does it HAVE to be a CAT?
So, instead of my cool, awesome CRUSADER CAT, the editors at LOCUSTS COMICS would prefer a DOG (more sales potential). So here I am, re-doing my comic...
You might think of this as selling out, but look, it sure beats drawing COCKS for the rest of my life.
Meow?
I know, Tobey... I know...

z z
z z Z z z z z z
z z z z Z z z
z z z z z z

-snore-
Hey, WAKE UP!
?
Do you mind telling us who-- or WHAT you are, friend?
...

Start talking, friend --

Okay, Ethan--this has GOT to be a FUCKIN' dream! Just wake up! Wet the bed if you have to!!
--otherwise, my colleague here will have to reintroduce you to his BLADE. Now SPEAK UP--what ARE you?!
He looks like a hairless ape. Maybe he's a mutant from New Primate.
Perhaps. Is that it, PAL? You some sort of mutant sent here to destroy us?!
shhh...
Uh...
YOU THOUGHT YOU COULD ESCAPE FROM ME, CRUSADER?!
And the day just got WEIRDER...

YOU AND I HAVE SOME UNFINISHED BUSINESS!!
You were once a HERO, Galen! But now you've been reduced to a pathetic HAS-BEEN! You've endangered this ENTIRE CITY over your bruised EGO!!
I've given more to this world than you could FATHOM with that peanut-sized brain! Yet my legacy is but a footnote in history-- unlike YOU, feline! YOU with your grandstanding heroics-- your GIFTS!
Gifts you never had to EARN!
I may have been BORN with special abilities--but I've proven myself worthy of them!
YOU'RE A TRAITOR, GALEN!
...a traitor, Galen...
OH. MY. GOD. I--I WROTE this. Word for word...

This is Crusader's grand battle. He's supposed to die while fighting Galen-- who's fueled by both jealousy and RAGE.
Everything is according to script--right down to the bystander's glasses. And if everything pans out the way I wrote it...
...Crusader's in trouble!
SHITBALLS!

GOOD GOD. HE'S
SOME KIND OF
SUPERBEING...
That--that was AMAZING. What are you? A mutant? An ALIEN?
At least tell us your name, friend...
Okay, Ethan. This is kinda surreal. You're trapped in a world of your own creation where you have SUPERPOWERS! Handle this with some grace...
YOU BITCHES CAN CALL ME ETHAN THE INCREDIBLE!

DAILY PURR
25 CENTS
ETHAN IS HERE
EXCLUSIVE PHOTOS INSIDE
EXTRA! EXTRA! READ ALL ABOUT OUR NEWEST AND GREATEST HERO-- ETHAN!!
Is it selfish of me to exploit these new powers? Perhaps... But I must have been brought here for a reason, right?
Heck--one might even say that I've been... CHOSEN.
ETHAN #1
ETHAN
Chosen to RID this city of EVIL! (Jeez, does EVERY villain in town own a giant robot suit?)

ETHANMANIA is currently sweeping the entire nation! Recent polls have indicated that Ethan is more popular than the Cat-President, the Cat-Pope, even CAT-JESUS!
CAT 7
Hey, as far as I'M concerned--this guy is the GENUINE ARTICLE. He's not even a CAT, but he's stepping up to protect all of us.
ETHAN
I--I've made this composite of what our KITTENS would look like. They're just absolutely precious, aren't they?
For a reasonable price of $49.99--you too can own KARATE CHOP ETHAN! Ask your parents, kits!
I will beat him to death with his own LIMBS! He will PAY for HUMILIATING the NAZI SWINE! He does have pretty nice hair, though...
I'M PRESENTING MYSELF TO ETHAN!

Today's guest needs no introduction. Folks, please give a warm welcome--
--to ETHAN!
Thanks so much for having me, OPURR.
CLAP
CLAP
CLAP
CLAP CLAP
CLAP
CLAP
The pleasure is all mine. So tell us about yourself, Ethan--
CLAP
CLAP CLAP
--shall we start with your mysterious origin, perhaps?
Well, it's all covered in my new hardcover, "Ethan: An Incredible Life." I'm the last son of a distant RED PLANET that exploded some time ago. My father, a brilliant scientist, sent me here on a ROCKET SHIP when I was but an infant.
I was raised in secrecy by my adoptive cat-parents, the ones who found my ship after it crashed. Exposure to your yellow sun has imbued me with these amazing gifts--gifts I use to PROTECT this fair city.
ETHAN
Well, we're CERTAINLY glad to have you--
CLICK
That story made absolutely no sense...

I know this may seem UN-VEGAN-- beating up anthropomorphic animals. But hey--I only beat up the EVIL ones.
Besides, I'm doing good work here. I finally have a significant purpose in this universe...
Everyone here appreciates me. I've managed to do in DAYS what Crusader NEVER accomplished -- turn CATROPOLIS into a UTOPIA.
And check out my new digs-- sure beats the cramped apartment in Williamsburg. I mean, look, who KNOWS how long I'll be stuck in this world. I might as well try to enjoy it here while I can...
...right?

MOM!!
I WANT ETHAN! DA ONE WIT KARATE CHOP ACTION, MOM!
Please, sir, there's NOTHING you can do? Look, look--I've got CASH!
-SOB-
-SOB-
Wish I could help ya, MA'AM. Gotta wait fer the next order.
SOLD OUT
SOLD OUT
BILL
Here, CHAMP! Have this complimentary CRUSADER CAT. I'm overstocked as it is...
CRUSADER SUCKS, DUDE!
SWEETIE!
HE'S LAME! HE DON'T EVEN GOT POWERS NOW!
Apologize RIGHT now, son!

TOY B

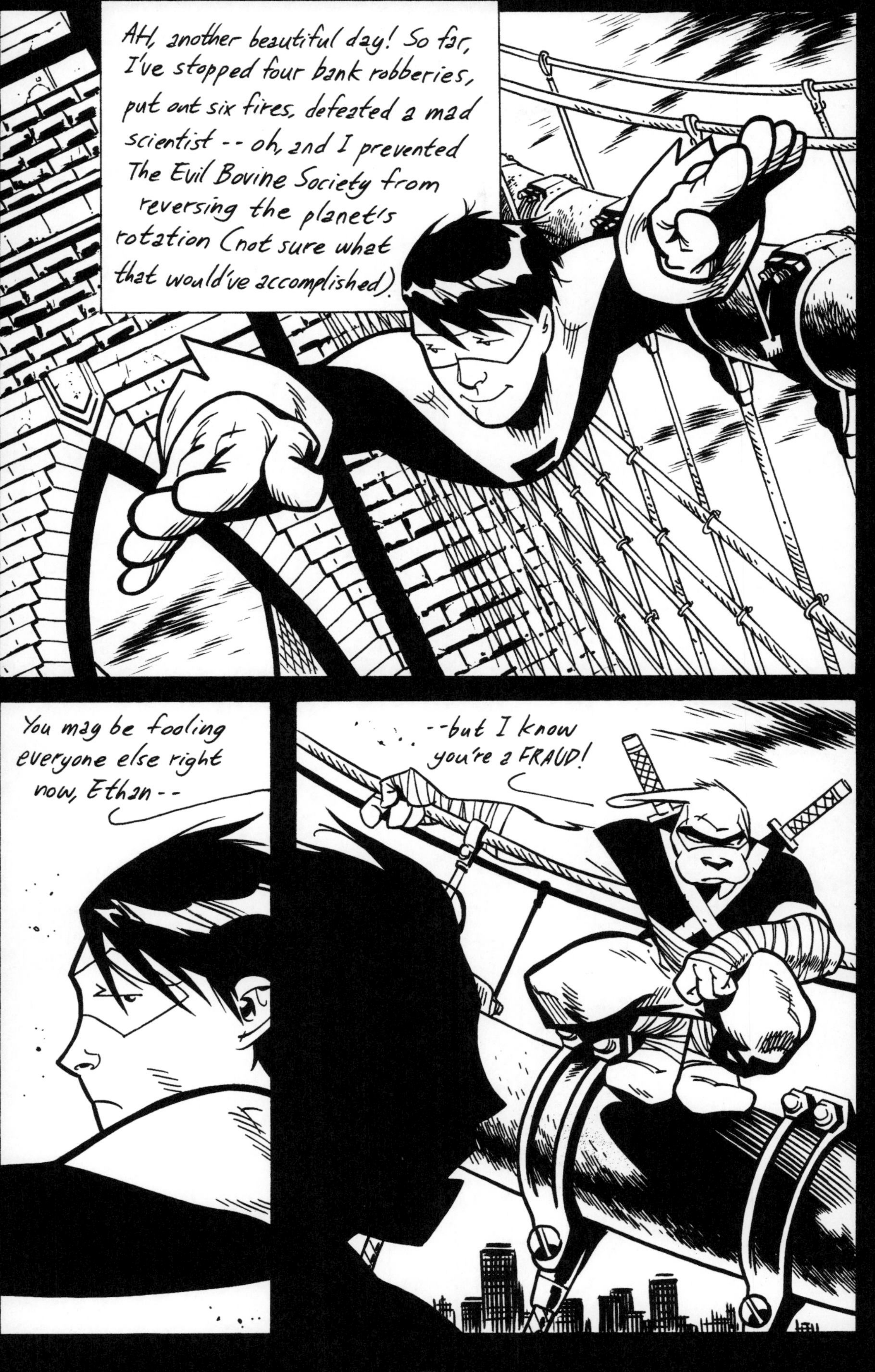
AH, another beautiful day! So far, I've stopped four bank robberies, put out six fires, defeated a mad scientist -- oh, and I prevented The Evil Bovine Society from reversing the planet's rotation (not sure what that would've accomplished).
You may be fooling everyone else right now, Ethan --
--but I know you're a FRAUD!

Ha, I'm not sure I've ever seen you without your rabbit, Mr. Hound. I've gotta say, your remarks sounded a bit HOSTILE there. I mean, come on--we're all on the same team, aren't we?
You're on NOBODY'S team! You've clearly demonstrated that you're nothing but a GLORY HOG, Ethan! All you care about is the constant attention and the fancy BOOK DEALS!
One must wonder what you must've been like BEFORE you decided to 'GRACE' us with your presence.
Watch your mouth, HOUND. Need I remind you that I saved your LIFE recently?
I suggest you back off--
Um...
--HEY! Are you even LISTENING to me?!

POW!
HOLY...
...CRAP!

...okay...
...that was UNCALLED for...
Hey, Sweetie...
...did you miss MOI?

GET AWAY, DEMON!
HOUND!
What the FUCK are you even DOING here?!!
You didn't really expect to hide in your adolescent comic world forever, did you?

CHIEF!!

CRUSADER?! WHAT ARE YOU EVEN DOING HERE?!!
We may not have any SUPERPOWERS, but Rabbit X and I are here to help in any way we can!
It's you stupid costumed types that CAUSED all this, you MORON!

CHIEF, WAIT! AT LEAST TELL US WH--
LOOK, I'M BUSY TRYING TO KEEP A BRIDGE FROM COLLAPSING! I DON'T EXACTLY HAVE TIME TO WASTE!
Come on, Rabby!
We can still he--
OUCH.

-cough-
SWEET JESUS, WOMAN!
-cough-
Could you PLEASE stop hitting me for ONE SECOND ?!
You don't even fucking BELONG HERE!!
Oh, that's FUNNY, Ethan! I'M the one who doesn't belong here? That's PRICELESS.
You wanna hear a hilarious joke of MINE? "What did the GIRDER say to the FACE?"
It must be his evil sister!
I said it before and I'll say it again-- OUCH!

Oops, my bad. Did that sting? Not everyone is attuned to my special brand of humor. Maybe I should just give up the comedy altogether-- stop deluding myself...
That's sound advice, wouldn't you say? STOP DELUDING YOURSELF. Some people just aren't meant for great things...
...some are just sad, lonely, inadequate boys jumping around in their silly pajamas. I almost PITY you...
Y-Yeah? Well... YOU did this to me...
Oh, REALLY?
I wouldn't fuckin' BE like this if it weren't for you! YOU'RE the one who left ME-- you REMEMBER that?!

THIS IS YOUR FAULT, OKAY?!
MY FAULT?! And whose fault was it LAST time, Ethan? Your brother? Or was it your father? You'll have to excuse me, I lose track of all your different scapegoats.
LICK MY SHIT! YOU'RE JUST A DAMN FIGMENT OF MY IMAGINATION-- SO GO FUCK YOURSELF!!
You're right. I AM imaginary. This is YOUR world, after all. So tell me, then...
... why are you losing?

This... uh... makes us even then, huh?
?

Great... more surprises?
The sky lights up and you automatically blame ME?
What are those FREAKS up to NOW?
IF YOU'VE GOT AN EXPLANATION-- NOW'S THE TIME!

"This is all for the best, Ethan..."

...I should get going. My dad's not going to be thrilled when I tell him my plans. I should probably use flash cards, huh?
-ahem- Well, I'll call you later this week to pick up the cats. I'm sure you can't wait to get some of them off your hands...
Just... take care for now, Ethan. I mean that...
Don't look yet, but there's a hot girl coming up on your left...
I'm sure she's hot as all hell...

Jeez, man, cheer up already. Is this your ULTRA-EMO WEEK? Come on-- look at those TITS!
Yes, very nice...
Dude, so what-- we're just here to DRINK tonight?
Now THAT'S depressing. SPILL IT-- what's bugging you?
"If you really want to know, Ash..."

... I've got major issues with my EX that I didn't even realize could EXIST. Issues that probably require MASSIVE amounts of alcohol, hence our current location...

"And let me ask you this, Ash: Would you sacrifice your own artistic integrity for fame and glory? Because I would--and DID. I'm a sell-out."
"I screwed over my own baby--figuratively speaking. So...yeah, I'm a bit down at the moment. It's a lot to stomach all at once..."

It's not every day you wake up and realize you're an asshole...

Well, I still like you. Does that count?

"Yeah, it does, Ash. Thanks."
"It's nice to know that someone's still got my back..."

THEN...
...so what is her name? Jessica? Is she Chines-- oh, okay then... ...no, it'd just be nice...
Always remember that GRADES COME FIRST, okay? ALWAYS. ...okay, we'll see you soon, son... ...night night.
Patrick is very excited to see you when he comes back. He told me he even bought you a new toy--a very 'cool' one.

You miss him, don't you?
sure...
Son, if you have free time, try studying more and drawing less...
Listen, your father loves you very much. He just had a very hard day. Business has been bad recently. And when he sees you drawing... he gets very upset. He wants to make sure you succeed one day -- he DOES care about you.
It's... it's VERY hard to make a good living with drawing... BELIEVE me, son.
Please don't be so upset with him...
mmhmm...

-sob-
-sob-
-sniff-
...sorry, son...
-sniff-
GOD...
Mom, it's okay...
I'm okay...
POW!

NOW...
Doesn't look like much of a cat there...
LOCUSTS COMICS
CRUSADER PUG
#1
Yeah, well, they wanted a dog instead. People just don't care for cats, I suppose.
It's still a great piece of work, son.
Would you mind if I showed this to your father?
Why? So he can rip it to shreds? I doubt he wants to see how I'm 'wasting' my life.

Son, he still cares about your career, believe it or not. You just never TALK to him...
Well... with THAT said, I still stand by my position. Besides, Dad doesn't even 'GET' comics.
You might as well show him a BAG OF ROCKS. At least THAT will amuse him longer.
Now you're just being SILLY.
-----LONG SIGH-----
Look, MOM, just don't bother, okay?
Fine, you WIN. But could I at LEAST show your brother? In fact, you should give an extra copy to him.
Eh... whatever.
-SIGH-
If YOU like it, Mom, that's all I really care about. You're my #1 FAN.

Despite my potent cynicism on the surface, things have actually been looking UP for me these days.
As you've already discovered--my comic has finally been published. Yeah, GRANTED, it differs drastically from its original concept--but hey-- published is PUBLISHED.
And Crusader Pug has been selling well, too. I mean, not astronomically well, but well enough to justify its publication.
HA HA HA HA
blah BLAH blah blah b
ah BLAH Martha this
BLAH BLAH blah blah
lunch break over-blah
BLAH blah blah BLAH
never get soup blah
blah BLAH blah blah
But not everything in life has been smooth. Recently, my living situation has become a bit... IFFY.
Long story short: Brian recently moved to Paris to study abroad for a semester...
BON JOUR!
...so it's just been me and April in the apartment.
BLAH BLAH BLAH blah BLAH blah BLAH BLAH blah blah blah BLAH BLAH

I actually thought you and April were a couple when I first met you two. You guys were joined at the HIP...
Yeah, that would drive me into THERAPY. I know she's HOT, but NO.
Since I'd been feeling so uncomfortable in my own home, I wisely took the time to meet other tenants (which April recommended in the beginning, anyway). Merk, who is a journalist, lives two flights below me and just HAPPENS to be a pretty awesome fellow COMIC NERD.
We became friends based on a mutual DISDAIN for our boss. But now that we don't work together anymore, our friendship has kinda... lost its spark. We don't really have much in common. And April needs someone to talk AT, rather then talk WITH. You know what I mean?
Never move in with a friend if you VALUE the friendship at ALL. I learned that lesson the HARD way back in SAN FRAN.

Dude, your comic is GREAT, by the way. I'm going to tell all my coworkers to run out and BUY a copy--help feed your cats.
CRUSADER PUG
Thanks. Be sure to twist some arms if you have to.
But after reading this, I'm left wondering what the comic could've been like if your original concept was left intact. Who DOESN'T wanna see a cat in a ROBOT SUIT battle an evil turtle, right?
Heh... Yeah...
Any idea how you would have even ENDED that story?
NOT A CLUE, MAN...

In addition to making new friends, I've resuscitated my love life. This is Gwen, and she's an assistant editor over at Locusts Comics. We've been casually dating for about a month now. Mixing business with pleasure, how taboo...
I just finished it. You like?
She's also an illustrator who specializes in these very trippy, ornate, hyper-detailed drawings. (Which are kind of cool... I guess...)
We get along really, really well. It's nice to finally date someone who's into the same stuff I am. The one downside: her OBESE cat seems to HATE me.
OOF!!
THE DREADED BOOBA MAN!
Oh, it's ON, boy...

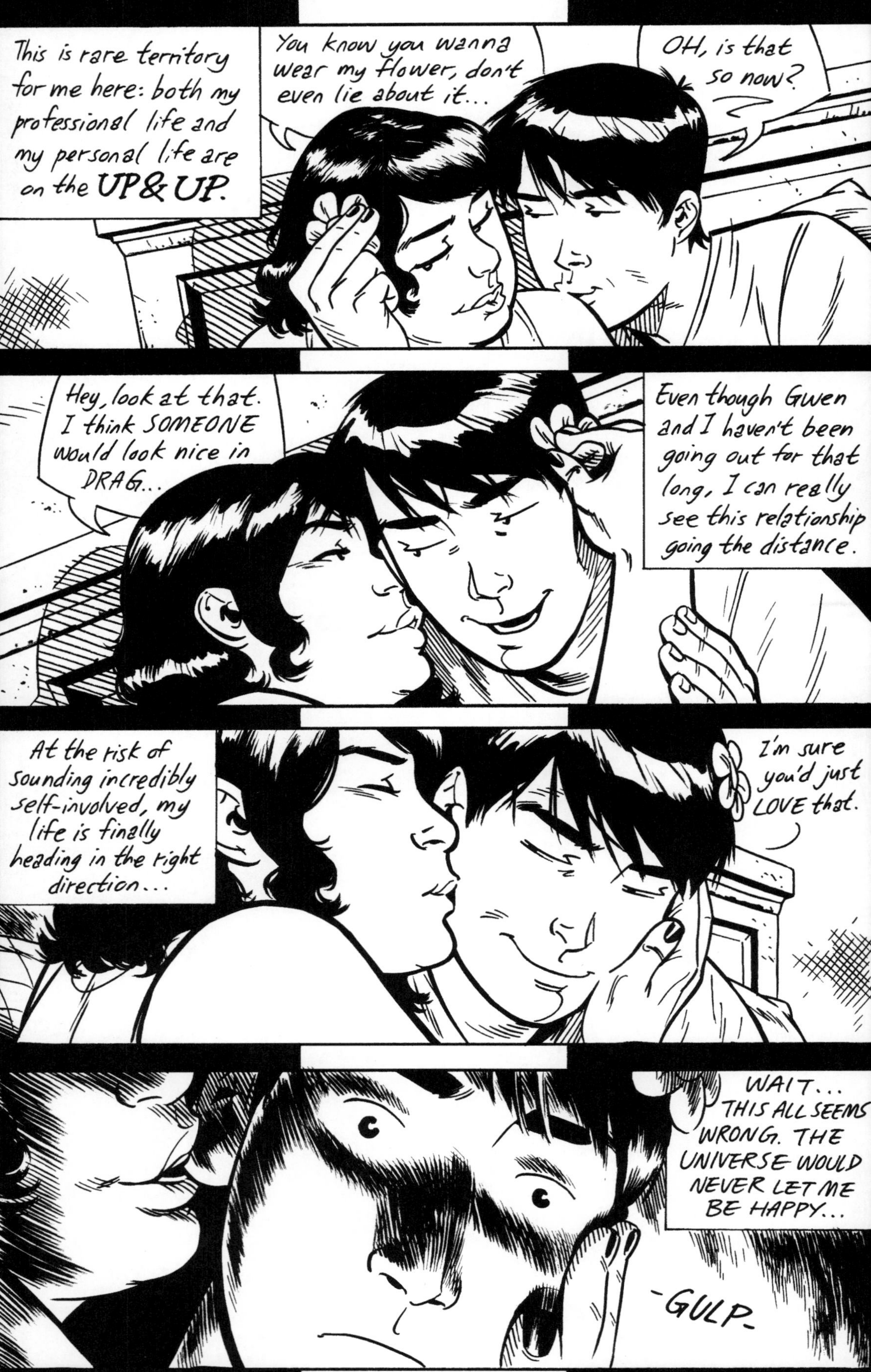
This is rare territory for me here: both my professional life and my personal life are on the UP & UP.
You know you wanna wear my flower, don't even lie about it...
OH, is that so now?
Hey, look at that. I think SOMEONE would look nice in DRAG...
Even though Gwen and I haven't been going out for that long, I can really see this relationship going the distance.
At the risk of sounding incredibly self-involved, my life is finally heading in the right direction...
I'm sure you'd just LOVE that.
WAIT... THIS ALL SEEMS WRONG. THE UNIVERSE WOULD NEVER LET ME BE HAPPY...
-GULP-

Shugie is all ready to go now. She last three of her back teeth, but now she'll be pain-free when she eats.
THREE TEETH?!
HUMANE SOCIETY of MANHAT
Not bad for a kitty her age -- especially when you consider she was a stray for so long.
PPPUURRRRRRRR
You'll need DENTURES soon, old lady...
When did you first take those cats in?
PPPUUURRRRRRRR
Since I left school. So... six years ago.
Or it might be seven years. I lose track.
Regretting that choice yet?
Would've saved a bundle on hairball medicine.
Eh, it ain't so bad in the end.
They keep the mice away.

Remember, don't feed her before eight o'clock tonight. Only water for now.
Sure thing, Dr. Brown.
I'll give you some extra meat tonight, baby.
MEOW.
Hey, you're still here. Shugie doing okay?
Oh... hey. Yeah, she is.
And here comes THE GREAT WALL OF BLAH.
BLAH BLAH got back from lunch just blah
BLAH BLAH blah BLAH
blah met this cute guy at book BLAH
BLAH you'd like
comic artist BLAH
blah blond hair
his book
Need to find a way to get out of here quickly.
BLAH blah BLAH BLAH
DRINKS THIS WEEKEND
BLAH BLAH bring Gwen
blah West Village
blah BLAH blah BLAH
So, you in?
HUH?
Uh, sure. Okay.
I've gotta go now. I've got... hemorrhoids.

99¢STORE
CAT

I know you must be satisfied with these numbers, Ethan...
We're thinking of soliciting the trade paperback early to get it in stores by the holiday rush.
MY LIFE
CRUSADER
Ha... it's nice to know that dropping out of school hasn't destroyed my immediate future yet.
Yeah, smart career move.
And speaking of which, that reminds me...
...I just picked this up. You seen it yet?
Um... what is it?

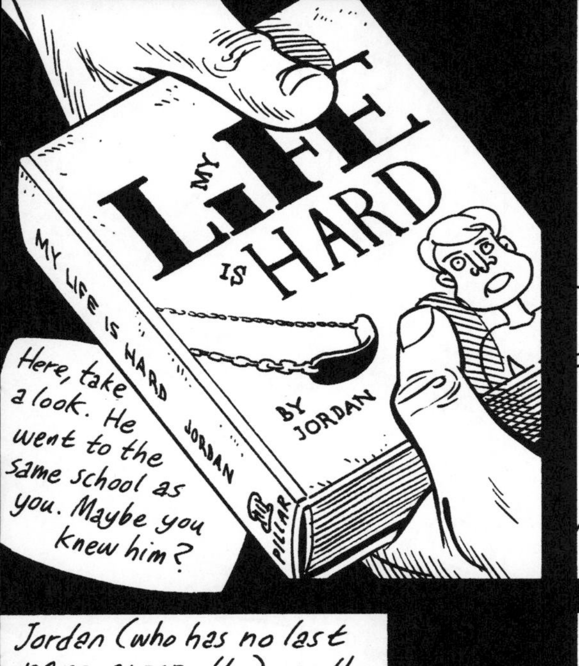
MY LIFE IS HARD
BY JORDAN
MY LIFE IS HARD JORDAN
PILLAR
Here, take a look. He went to the same school as you. Maybe you knew him?

It's not a bad read. You can borrow it if you want. Looks like you're both doing well these days.
JORDAN?! Oh, you've gotta be FUCKIN' with me!
MY

Jordan (who has no last name, apparently) was the pretentious blowhard that every art class seemed to have. The kind of guy who cared more about his HAIR than his CRAFT.

And MAN--don't get me started on this guy's 'ART.' Of all the aspiring artists I've known throughout my life, Jordan was the ULTIMATE HACK. Yet he strutted around campus like he was GOD'S GIFT to pencil and paper.

TODAY IS THE FIRST DAY OF THE REST OF MY LIFE.

What's even worse was how he JUSTIFIED it...
My work is less about FORM, and more about the PURE ESSENCE of drawing.
Sure, Jordan...

...but everyone else ate his shit up with a spoon: classmates, teachers, EVERYONE.
Thank you, thank you, you're too kind...

And now he's been PUBLISHED?! HE--UGH--OH NO! NOT NOW!
MY LIFE
I'VE KEPT HIM DORMANT...
I MUSN'T RELEASE...
...THE INCREDIBLE ETHAN!
LIFE
ETHAN? Are you INSANE?

THEN...
Dude, draw some kind of sword there--
PUBLIC 2 SCH
--one with SPIKES and a giant handle!
MILK
No, no, that's GAY, man. Give him a big LASER GUN instead!
Yeah, like THAT!
Ethan...
...I need to speak with you for a moment.
I need you to be honest with me, okay? Don't lie.
...

These marks on your face... did Jerome pick on you? The boy from Mr. Li's class.
You don't have to be afraid to tell me. I know that Jerome has picked on some of the Chinese children before. Was it him, Ethan?
Yeah...
Okay. You can go back to your drawing.
You're very, very talented, son. I hope your art teacher is encouraging you to keep it up. It's a rare gift.

NOW...
MARS
So tell me, man, how'd you become such an old cat lady after college?
It's a very long story. I doubt you'd be interested.
Who here enjoys irony? Show of hands...
April is DATING Jordan! To say that it's a 'SMALL WORLD' would be an EPIC UNDERSTATEMENT!
Apparently, they met at one of Jordan's NUMEROUS book signings last month. I'm sure it was love at first sight. (-SCOFF-)

Hey, this guy's got a big heart. He's Schindler-- but with CATS.
Thanks, Ash. That's not laying it on too thick at ALL.
No, I love animals. I had dogs growing up. But six CATS just seems a bit EXTREME to me.
Hey, at least the cats provide some inspiration, right, Ethan?
...mmhmm...
I'm glad to see that you've been published, Ethan...
...I always wondered if you'd make it or not.

Even though it TOOK you long enough. Haha. But look, in all seriousness, if you want to take your career to the next level-- GET AN AGENT. The right agent can be the difference between getting a book deal at LOCUSTS, or--
SHUT YOUR BIG MOUTH AND TAKE OFF THAT PRETENTIOUS SCARF!!
--getting one at PILLAR. Trust me on this--AGENT!
Thanks...
I'll look into it...

COMICS
CRUSADER PUG IS THE BEST DAMN COMIC I EVER READ!
UGH -- ASH, we're in a COMIC SHOP...
GUID
Look, it's not that I don't appreciate all the support. Just try to tone it down.
Dude, I'm just injecting your comic with the publicity that it clearly needs!
MANGA
-SIGH-
So...you have as much FUN as I did last night?
God, I've NEVER, EVER seen you so passive-aggressive. How did you NOT anticipate seeing Jordan? I'm assuming that April at least TOLD you the name of her new boyfriend, right?

Maybe next time she should check to see if I'm actually LISTENING.
Fine, then it's your fault. At least we didn't have to pay.
Hey, HEY, you want to read an AWESOME comic?
Buy Crusader Pug. It's got it all.
Oh, thanks. I haven't seen this comic yet. The cover looks cool.
Any thing else you'd recommend?
NAH-- by comparison, all other comics are CRAP.
FROM THE CREATORS OF CRAP
GUILD
THANKS...
Do I collect my commission NOW or LATER?
GUILD

OHMYGOD...
...you're ACTUALLY crying to TERMINATOR 2?! I thought men crying to T2 was nothing but a MYTH.
It's that DAMN T-800. He's the BEST HERO EVER.
"I know now why you cry... but it's something I could never do."
HA HA HA HA HA HA HA HA HA HA HA HA HA HA HA HA
GEE, I'm sorry this isn't 'My Life is Hard.'
W-WAIT, you didn't like Jordan's book -- but you CRY for T2?
TERMINATOR 2 is about FAMILY! It's about the connection between Sarah and John -- between John and the Terminator. This story has SUBSTANCE, regardless of the fact that it's an ACTION FILM.

Whereas JORDAN'S book... is nothing more than quasi-intellectual CHICKEN SCRATCH.
So, by YOUR standards, I'm considered a chicken scratch fan?
Well, you know, you DID enjoy 'CRASH,' sweetie. I mean... COME ON.
Okay, since we're being so HONEST here, lemme ask you... what do you think of MY work?
...yeah, you know I like your work, sweetie...
Um...
RING TONE
WHY, LOOK AT THAT, IT'S MY PHONE. I BETTER PICK IT UP, COULD BE IMPORTANT.
Not off the hook, BUSTER.
RING TONE

Hello? Oh, hey, Mom. Where are you calling me from? I didn't recogniz--
--WAIT. Slow down, Mom. What happened, exactly?
I SAID--your father had a STROKE. We're at PACE HOSPITAL right now.
I've already phoned Patrick. He's leaving work early and driving straight here. Where are you right now, son?
When can you make it down here?
SON?

THEN...
That thing is LIMITED edition, man. Every store was practically sold out.
And be careful with it, okay? That toy's going to be worth a BUNDLE one of these days.
Okay...

Look, man, I know how you're feeling. Dad was never too kind to me either. It was even WORSE back in China. Growing up there was like being in JAIL- and that's not even a joke.
Dad doesn't know any better. HIS father was a major PRICK, so now Dad is the way he is. It's not fair to any of us, I know. No use in crying about it.
And Mom isn't going to help either. She can barely stand on her own anymore. You have to learn to be strong, don't let any of this SHIT get under your skin. The sooner you get that, Ethan, the BETTER.
Okay?
Okay...
This arm's kinda loose...

NOW...
Since when do you smoke?
Doing it to be cool?
And I suppose you all smoke for the HEALTH benefits?
HA. That's actually kinda funny.
Anyhoo, put down the cheap whiskey and come to MARS LOUNGE with us. Jordan's treat again.

No, thanks. Not in the mood.

You guys have fun with Jordan.

OH, BOY. What is it THIS time, Ethan? GIRL TROUBLE? Lemme guess-- Gwen isn't turning out to be the MATCH MADE IN HEAVEN that you were hoping for-- am I right?

GEE, April--maybe I just don't want to hang out in some YUPPIE lounge with that EMPTY-HEADED BOY TOY of yours! Infact--I have to question the character of anyone who is even REMOTELY impressed by Jordan's BIG BAG OF BULLSHIT!

HOW'BOUT IT, APRIL?!

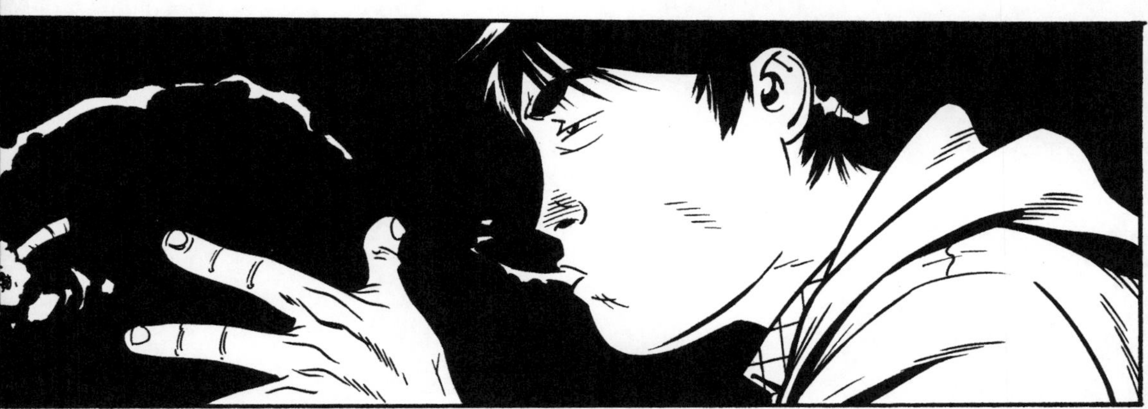

That stuff won't solve your troubles...

Yeah? Well, it's a WONDERFUL distraction...
...and WHO are you?
The name's FRANK C.
Pleased to make your acquaintance, Ethan...

Canarsie, Brooklyn
God, look at all this shit...
LANA! Jesus, get out of there before you knock stuff down!
RING TONE
Here, go play with Clarkie.
Let's see who it is, Lil' Bub.
...
Hey-- what's up? Been a while...
Yeah, it has. Um... so how are you?
Oh, uh...

...just clearing out my grandpa's old shit from the second floor. Planning to move down here soon. The cats are going nuts with all the extra space.
So, uh, how's YOUR bunch doing these days? Everyone is healthy, I assume?
Oh, you know... eating, sleeping, pooping... the usual stuff...
OH--I did run into that friend of yours from Holyoke... um... Penny, or something. On a blind date. What was she doing in New York, even?
You mean Penelope. She transferred to NYU over the summer.
Nobody can really survive a full FOUR years living in South Hadley. She wanted to do some volunteer work, so I pointed her towards the shelter.
But yeah, I DID hear about that blind date. Apparently, April told Penelope that you worked in finance.
Oh, that fucker...

Ethan... I'm not looking to be rude, but... what was your reason for calling tonight? Not, you know, that I'm not glad...
...I wanted to ask you something...

DUDE--I don't know HOW you know my fucking name...
Just... leave me alone and FUCK OFF, okay?

Heh... ever the charmer, eh? Listen to me, little man, I normally don't do this. In fact, I'm not supposed to do this. I'm more of a BEHIND-THE-SCENES kind of guy. But--seeing as how you're so down on yourself this evening--I found it prudent to intervene.
And trust me, I'm not fuckin' with you here. Not ONE BIT. I'm on the level, all right?

I said 'FUCK OFF'-- not 'START RANTING.'
SO... FUCK OFF THEN.

Hey, I know what a guy like you wants. You want Jordan's life...

He's got a very impressive life-- the kind of life that YOU'VE always wanted to achieve, yeah?
Jordan's got mild fame, a fistful of cash, and the pick of any hipster chick he desires. I can make it so that YOU have that perfect life, man. NO STRINGS ATTACHED. I'm 100% LEGIT on this. You deserve it, don't you? After all this time...

HA!! April put you up to this SHIT, didn't she?! GOD, THE NERVE OF THAT FUCKIN' WOMAN!!

Think on it, Ethan. This is the only time an offer like this'll come along.
You can finally make him proud of you...

LOOK, FUCKHEAD-- YOU CAN GO AHEAD AND SUCK MY DI--
"Was I a terrible boyfriend?"
What I mean is... do you have any major regrets? With US? If you could go back in time and change everything... WOULD you?
ETHAN...
NO, NO, this isn't about getting back together. Sorry if that was confusing. This is just a personal question.
Well, we've certainly had our share of... interesting times. But that doesn't mean that I would ever change it.
We had some good times, too, right?

Yes. Yes, we did. Besides, where would we be if we weren't a pair of old cat ladies? We'd be normal. Who wants THAT, huh?
Heh... not me.
-ahem- Well, uh, I guess I'll let you go now, Sin...
Yeah... I should get back to cleaning. Got a lot of boxes here...
You... you take care, okay?
I will...

PACE HOSPITAL
ZZZZZZ
mom...
I had a very long night. Sorry.
It's okay, son, no need to be sorry. It was a long night for all of us.
Yeah, I see that. Are you hungry at all? Coffee?
Not at the moment, son.

So what's the damage?
The doctor said it was a TIA, so just a 'mini-stroke.' He's okay, with all things considered.
He needs to stop smoking, obviously.
Are YOU okay, Mom?
I am. I was very anxious at first, but Patrick was here to help.
ZZZZZZZZZZ

CRUSADER PUG
I'm very glad that you came, son. Thank you...
No problem, Mom.

PACE HOSPITAL

3A
"Yeah, it's time to start looking for a new place..."

It's a done deal, huh? You sure you don't wanna try and talk some of these things out with April?
Nah, you know how it is. It's been a long time coming. This recent thing with Jordan was just a catalyst.
Also, I think Ash is still upset with me, too. It's a whole mess, really.
-sigh- I'm sorry I'm bugging you with all of this. I'm just not looking forward to apartment hunting.
Hmm, maybe I can move in with Gwen... (NO, NO, BAD IDEA)
I ever tell you what happened with me in San Fran?
Not much about it, no...

I was totally in love with my roommate then, Thora. She was smart, funny, cute. She was also a journalism major, so she was a girl I could talk shop with. When I finally confessed my feelings-- I got shot down.
Thora said she didn't want to ruin our friendship. I thought things would still be cool between us, but Thora became... cold and distant. She would dart into her room whenever there was a mere sighting of me. We barely nodded.
I packed up all my stuff and bounced-- WITHOUT saying goodbye. What was the point, right? I ended up crashing on friends' couches for months in a row.
Mark... if this story is going where I THINK it's going, let me reiterate my position one last time: I AM NOT IN LOVE WITH APRIL. I don't see HOW your story relates...
Ethan, just let me finish. There IS a point...
This was a VERY SHITTY period in my life. After months of couch surfing, I landed with my buddy, Thomas, who was an all-around nice guy.
One day, Tom gets a call from his dad in Ohio.

Tom's mother had been diagnosed with ovarian cancer. I met his mom once--she was a great lady. Tom was devastated. He flew home to be with his family and left me the apartment for that weekend, all to myself. And I did some thinking...
There I was, moping on a fold-out couch, feeling bad for myself because a girl had rejected me. And meanwhile, my friend was having REAL problems-- REAL issues.
I'm...really, really sorry to hear about your friend's mom...
I was, too...
I made a choice-- to get my life back on track. To be ME again.
That's all life really is, man. A series of choices.

Goodnight,
Shugie...

Sweet dreams...

WELCOME
CITY

Ratso LOVES it when you run, little bunny. Your sweat and fear make the KILL that much sweeter...

YOU SCARED, LITTLE BUNNY?!
Hehe. I think he IS, Ratso. I bet he's CRYIN' under them goggles!

Your move, little bunny. Ain't NOWHERE you can dash where Ratso won't FIND YA...
Come on, then...
Let me BUST that other eye out for you!
Ethan, you there?

Did you not get enough sleep? Or am I boring you to death?
You've got to pay attention here, Ethan. Do you need some coffee to wake yourself up?
I'm sorry...sorry, Hank. I didn't get much sleep last night. Stayed up to finish the page in time and bring it in...

Ethan, it's a DOG-EAT-DOG world out there. Being tired is no excuse.
You've got to SHOW me your commitment here.
mmhmm...
Meet Hank Scott, a successful stockbroker and aspiring comic writer.
At age forty, Hank feels that the comics field is ripe for him to conquer. Like everyone else jumping on the comics bandwagon, Hank's got 'GREAT IDEAS' but doesn't draw, which is why I'm sitting here.
This panel here -- it needs more emotional content. That's what comics are ALL about, okay?
mm hmm...
Quite frankly, I wouldn't have taken this gig unless I really, REALLY needed the paycheck.
It's been three months since I moved out of Williamsburg. After that debacle with April, it became clear that I wasn't what you'd call 'roommate material'. I moved down to Crown Heights, which is further away from the city than the 'burg, but provides cheaper digs.
23
REAL ESTATE
PHONE

I found this two-room studio for me and the cats. It was the cheapest place that I could find that was both pet-friendly and NOT the size of a closet. Rent is still a bit much (we are in NYC, after all), which is why I took the job with Hank.
Oh, which reminds me, you wanna take a look at Hank's 'GREAT IDEA'?
X-MEN
THEY STOLE MY LIFE AND MADE ME A FREAK. NOW IT'S PAYBACK TIME!!
It's called 'Killer Max X,' the tale of a government labrat who escapes and wages war on his totalitarian masters. (I know, it's WILDLY original, right?)
I ♡ CHICKS
NO DUDES
SERIOUSLY, I'M NOT GAY
Actually, it's not the project ITSELF that frustrates me -- it's HANK.

When the movie deals come pouring in, you're going to be a RICH man, Ethan. We're going to grab the comics world by the BALLS. You give me 110%, and I'll take us the rest of the way!
mmm...
Why don't you try to look on the bright side? You're making a GREAT page rate now-- a PROFESSIONAL page rate, okay?
CURLY
VEGETARIAN
CAFE
SEITAN CUBANO
Most young artists would KILL to be in your position. TRUST me--I work with them, week to week.

Yeah, extra cash at this time is GREAT, don't get me wrong. But you've just gotta MEET Hank. He's so ALPHA-MALE, MACHO, WALL STREET.
PLUS, he knows SHIT about comics...
Tell you what, Ethan... don't WANT the job? I know, like, twelve other illustrators who'd give their left testicle to take the project.
If it seems like Gwen is being a bit... BLUNT with me, it's because things have been sorta rocky as of late.
DEAL?
-sigh-
You see, Gwen recommended moving in together while I was still apartment hunting. I felt that it was too soon. I know that sounds like such a typical 'guy' cliché, but it really WAS too soon. We haven't even reached a YEAR yet.

Also--and this isn't a joke--
I think her cat, Booba-Man,
is trying to MURDER me in
my sleep. There is NO WAY
that HER cat and MY cats
could peacefully coexist.
I've explained this to Gwen,
but it only seems to upset
her more. Honestly, I think
there's another strong,
underlying reason why Gwen
has been so pissed lately...

The Crusader Pug TPB
didn't sell particularly well.
I felt the staff at Locusts
(Gwen included) could've
done a much better job
at promoting the trade on
the book market. Instead,
'Crusader Pug: Volume One'
simply faded into the mix
with every other funny
animal comic. Gwen thinks
I'm still harboring a little
resentment. No comment.

-ahem- Anyway, so here
I am, sitting through
one of Gwen's awkward
silent treatments.
Good times...
So... how 'bout
them KNICKS,
huh?

Also, Gwen's birthday is just around the corner. God, I really suck at gift shopping. Would it be wrong to just hand her one of my cats?
Harnes & N
s & Nobel
Let's see here, Gwen and I have exactly the same interests: comics, TV, and movies. This shouldn't be too hard.
Poetry
Graphic N
Eh, since I'm here, I might as well check up on how a certain graphic novel is selling these days...
LiFE HARD
LiFE HARD
BAT BOY
50% OFF
Well, it's like Gwen said, at least I've got work... right?

ELSEWHERE...
They got Rabbit X! If HE'S dead, then the rest of us are the EASY PICKINGS!
We don't know if he's dead yet, Tex.
Who are we kidding?! He was probably fed to the KOMODO by now!!
SHUT YOUR MOUTH! You're scaring the little ones.
I thought HOUND killed the KOMODO.
Care to share anything?

Jordan was cheating on April the whole time?
Ash and I managed to 'make up' last month. This is the first time we've really hung out since I bolted from April's apartment. I've yet to mend things with April, but Ash keeps me in the loop.
I think it was with TWO different girls, also.
SON OF A BITCH.
Dude, and you should SEE April now. She's been eating her emotions and she's beginning to look PLUMP. She's starting to resemble a daddy longlegs spider.

Kinda serves her right with that FREAKISH metabolism of hers. I love CRUEL IRONY.
Jeez, what do you do-- stash a secret voodoo doll underneath your pillow at night?
Look, man, you never had to LIVE with her. The incessant smartass remarks aren't as 'cute' when it's 24/7. It's fuckin' EXHAUSTING!
Well, all's fair, I guess. You wouldn't want to hear what April says about YOU. -SIP-
...
What? What is she saying? I wanna know. Is it as bad as DADDY LONGLEGS?
You really want to know?
SPILL THE SOYBEANS.
OKAY...

Ethan likes to think of himself as some kind of **AUTEUR,** but 'Crusader Pug' is sophomoric trash. "Oh, but it's ironic." Sure, whatever.
-CHOMP- And he's so EFFIN' jealous of Jordan, it's not even funny. At least Jordan isn't a sellout, even if he IS a sleazy, two-timing **ASS**. Watch--Ethan will be doodling GAY PORN for the rest of his LIFE.

...BITCH...

Hey, don't DISH it if you can't TAKE it, buddy. Besides, why would you give a SHIT what April says about you? You're successful.

You're an artist that EATS! And you earn WAY more than April. He who laughs LAST, laughs BEST! Am I right?

LOLITA
"Remember--
EMOTIONAL
CONTENT."
WE NEED TO
DEFUSE THIS
BOMB! NOW!
God, I need
some fresh
air...

Hey... wait a second...

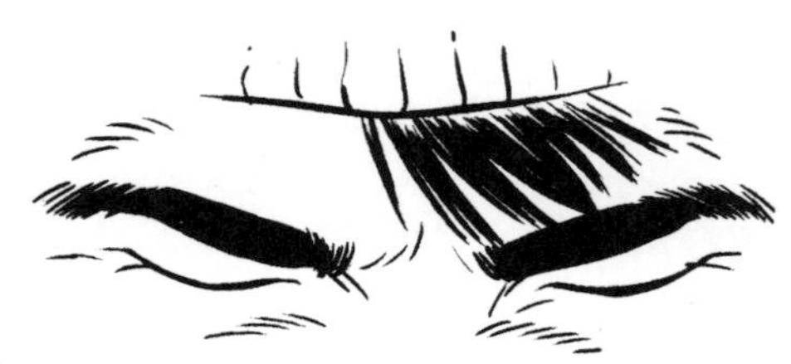

AW, FUCK ME...

You always manage to appear when things are at their worst, Ethan.
We really could've USED you these past TEN YEARS...
W--WHAT?

After the incident on Catropolis Bridge, the villains of this city, and EVERY city, joined forces in an attempt to take over the world.
Without YOU around, and with ME depowered, we simply didn't stand a chance. City after city collapsed. Catropolis was our last stand.
We did everything we could, but in the end... we lost.

Actually, we were FLAT-OUT **ANNIHILATED,** if we're aiming to be HONEST here. It's a darn shame that you weren't around.
Yeah, it was a nice little PARADISE you left for us, HERO.
TRIGGER! FAYE! STOP this before I stop it FOR you! Ethan is NOT the enemy here.
No, you're right, Crusader-- let's throw him a GIANT PARADE!

Let's all go easy on the HAIRLESS APE who RUINED our lives. None of this craziness started until HE showed up a DECADE ago! HE'S the reason we have to live like this! HE'S the reason RABBIT X is DEAD!!
Rabbit X? He's DEAD?
We don't know. Not for sure, anyway. Rabbit X went missing around two weeks ago.
We were actually in the middle of another sweep before we ran into you. So far, no luck.
Yo, speaking of which, we really need to be heading back. This ain't the best place to hold your reunion.
Come on.
You ride in the back.

COMFY?
Well, well... look who's come back to play...

So, Rabbit X and Faye, are they, like...?
His daughter.
Oh, oh... I didn't realize he had a family and stuff...
HAD, yes. His wife died during the war.

She was absolutely the FINEST marksman I'd ever met.
Next to me, of course.
Don't dwell on it, Ethan. Her death is not your fault.
-pfft-
FAYE...
No, actually, Faye's right. You SHOULD blame me, Crusader.
WHY?
You all needed me. You said it yourself, okay? I know you're doing your best to patronize me, but I KNOW when I've screwed up.
I mean, come on, I'M the one who gave up on YOU...
And all for a stupid pug...

PUG? WHAT PUG?

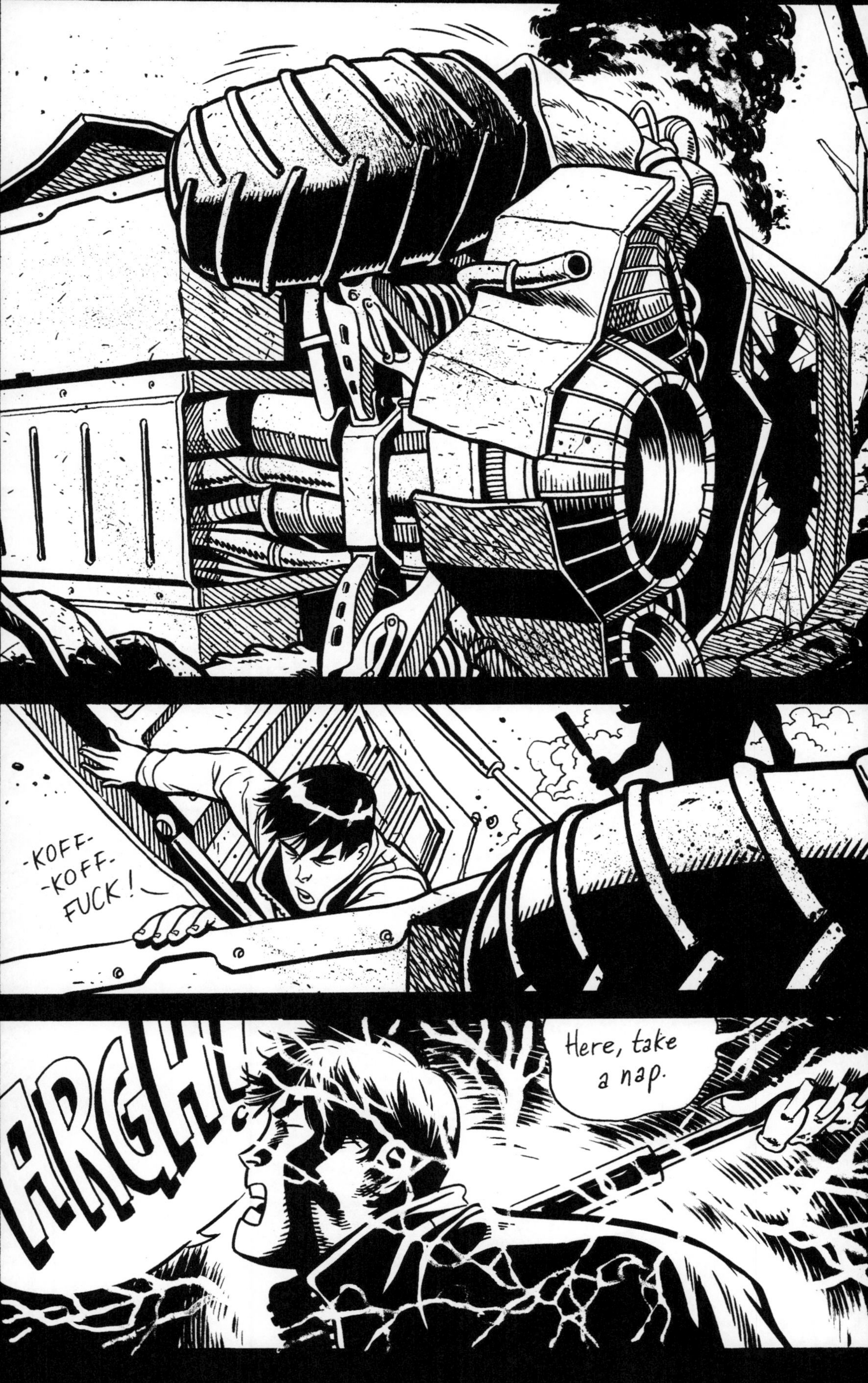
-KOFF-
-KOFF-
FUCK!
ARGH!
Here, take a nap.

Nah, Ratso, ain't NO WAY this the same guy. He s'pose to be INVULNERABLE! He's also TALLER, if I remember.
Maybe age has made him weaker. Ten years older, ten years slower.
So long as he's alive, the boss'll be pleased...
YES, INDEED. Hehe...

What about the rest of them?
Who cares? They're dead.
Ugh...
WRONG. MOVE. RATSO.

Ethan?
Man, is that really you?
You okay?

...Rabbit X? You're not dead...
Where... uh... where are we?
HELL, pretty much.
Oh... well... it's good to see you...
God, payback is SWEET indeed.

I love to see a hero crumble...
We did GOOD, eh, boss?
Yes, you did GOOD, Swine. VERY good...

We just got AMBUSHED and left for DEAD, Crusader!
METRO
Now you're suggesting we gather up and attack Galen's base?! And all for that HAIRLESS APE?!!
Actually, Faye, it was an ORDER-- one I expect you to FOLLOW.

Well, no offense, but I think we should listen to Faye this time.
We're not an army, we're just a band of families and survivors. You're asking too much.
We can't hide forever, Trigger.

I've known Galen longer than anyone. He will patiently wait us out--eradicate us one by one until our numbers collapse. I don't need to remind everyone here how successful his approach has been.
We have two clear options. The first option sounds the most sensible: HIDE. Hide and await the inevitable, yes? We'll all grow old together inside this cold, metal tube. OR...
Silenc
...we take a bold stand. We take this fight straight to Galen's doorstep.
A nice speech can't change the odds, Hound. Any way you cut it, it's still a SUICIDE MISSION. I've already lost my mother... AND my dad...
You think I've forgotten? BOTH were my friends--one was my PARTNER. All the more reason to AVENGE them.

Hound--can you even COMPREHEND how overpowered we are?
Well... then we better make this one count.
Right?
You want to take the point, old friend?
Absolutely.
Okay. Trigger, round up every single able body you can muster.
And bring me my gun... the BIG one.

I've met Faye, by the way. She's quite... bold.
Ha, she completely takes after her mother in that way.
However, I'M the one who taught her all those fighter moves. She can damn near kick anyone's ass.
Even YOU, maybe.
HMM...
So... listen. Whenever you're ready, let's BUST outta here and run like crazy.
What?
This is just a RUSE, isn't it? You get yourself captured, they bring you into the lair, and then we can AMSCRAY. You've got SUPERSTRENGTH. Just snap these chains already.
Run that by me again?

Um... well, see, here's the thing. I don't seem to HAVE any superpowers anymore. Not sure why. Trust me, if I did, we would've both been out of here the second I woke up.
Crap... does it have anything to do with your evil sister?
HUH?
MY WHAT?
Your evil sister. You fought her on the bridge a decade ago.
Oh... OH. (EWW)
SUUURE. We'll go with that.
-SIGH- Great, so we're essentially BONED.
We're going to die here, Ethan.

I'm tellin' ya, BOSS, we should OFF those two and get it over with!
Don't be a silly fool, Swine! You must learn to SAVOR the kill -- prolong it. Make them BEG for mercy. Quick deaths are NEVER satisfying.
Heh-- that's what RATSO's been tellin' the PIG all along.
Just SAYIN', is all.
"You don't simply take your enemy's LIFE, Swine -- you take their DIGNITY!"
"Did you take no joy or pleasure as you watched the fear BOILING in Crusader's eyes?"

Well... we just blasted their HIPPIE VAN. We didn't, you know, BEHEAD 'em or anything. But they looked dead to me.
Yeah, boss, they were already GONERS!
!
?
Hey, Gasol. Come take a look at this. What's it look like to you?

KNOCK. KNOCK.

THOSE FILTHY REBELS JUST SIGNED THEIR OWN BLOODY DEATH SENTENCE!
I WANT THE CAT MYSELF! I WANT HIS FLESH!
HEY--
KEYS... NOW...
I SMELL AN OLD HOUND.

You show great tenacity, Crusader. It is your defining attribute, without a doubt. I've never met a pesky feline so hard to KILL!
But sadly, you have a GLARING FLAW. Do you know what you lack?
-COUGH- My two front teeth? -COUGH-
You lack RESPECT-- RESPECT FOR THOSE IN POWER!
I'll have to educate you through BLINDING PAIN!

Quit YAPPIN' and bring it on, then!
-COUGH- I'm tired of this TICKLEFEST.

WE GET THROUGH THIS--YOU OWE ME A BEER!
Mouth off AFTER we get outta here, Trig!
IT'S TIME TO END THIS!

WHERE IS THE GERIATRIC DOG?!
Great...
...they've released the KOMODO.

What's happening out there?!
What do ya think?!

SCREW THIS! SCREW ALL OF IT!

Show some more effort, little bunny. Didn't you inherit your mom's SPIRIT? Heh... now THAT was a good kill.
Took Ratso's LEFT EYE with her, too. Now, let's see... what shall we cut off first? An ear? Maybe those cute little fingers of yours...

Point of advice, Ratso...
...speaking entirely in the third person makes you sound ridiculous. Rest in Hell, SLIME.
FAYE?! FAYE--OH GOD, ARE YOU OKAY THERE?!
D-Dad? You're ALIVE!
Yes, I am, sweetie. But are YOU okay? You're not seriously HURT, are you?
Of course I'm okay, Dad.
I got your moves...

So what's the EXIT PLAN here?
This IS the exit plan-- RUN!
The element of surprise was our only advantage. And we definitely didn't think that my DAD was still alive here. We basically --
--came here for ME.

DON'T SHOOT ME-- YOU'LL HURT MY FEELINGS!

NOW... LET'S KISS AND MAKE UP...
The dog could use some assistance...
It won't be long before KOMODO rips the HOUND in half to feast on his INNARDS. Pity...
Surrender is still an option, Crusader. You can either have a dignified death...
...or end up like your canine colleague down there--with your HEAD in my trophy room.
HAHAHA.

M-MASTER?!
MASTER!!
THIS AIN'T OVER YET, BOYS!
I SAY WE SKIN HIM ALIVE!
Care to say that to my FACE?
-GULP-

That was some loud bang.
THERE! We came in through THAT way!
You think -cough- you think you're so brave -- so heroic. Don't you, cat? You've taken down the big, BAD TURTLE.
Look--I think I see Hound!
Rabby?

But I always... ALWAYS remember to leave myself OUTS. That's why I'M the smart one, CAT.
HAHA HAHA
HAHA! SEE YOU IN HELL! HAHA HA
EVERYONE!!!
RUNNNN

NONONONONONO
NONONONONONO
ONONONONONO
NONONONONONON
ONONONONONON
ONONONONONON
NONONONONON
ONONONONON
NONONO

NOOOO

Why haven't you been answering your phone? I've been waiting outside your apartment for, like, ten minutes.

Birthday dinner, remember? Your boyfriend duties?
Sweetie...
I was just joking there.
. . .

JOHN
WAS
ZOMBIE WASTE

Um...

...COULD SOMEONE EXPLAIN TO ME WHAT THE **HELL** JUST HAPPENED?

Meanwhile ...
C442
Okaaaaay.

"This is the main villain here, Ethan, The SuperMegaLord. This panel really has to POP, okay? Focus on the EMOTIONAL CONTENT."
HA HA HA! YES! THE POWER IS ALL MINE!
"Yeah, sure, okay."
"And remember, MAX is EXTREMELY angry at this point. Be sure to work on the emotional--"
SURRENDER NOW, SUPERMEGALORD-- OR PREPARE TO BE DESTROYED!
"--emotional content, yes, I know, I know."

"Ethan, you're never going to make it in this BIZ if you can't take some constructive criticism. You should listen to me."
DESTROY ME?! WHY, MAX--AREN'T YOU EVEN AWARE THAT I'M...
... YOUR FATHER?!
"SURE."
"Man, with MY writing and YOUR art, which I will help you improve, this is going to be a HUGE HIT. It's what readers have been waiting for!"
"Mmm..."

You know those times... when you're absolutely sure you're right? When you think there's ZERO CHANCE of being proven wrong?
I expected Killer Max X to fail after two issues. I pictured Hank being laughed out of town...
Instead, Killer Max X became a sleeper hit. I mean, the first two issues actually SOLD OUT! Readers are eating up the 'obvious' self-parody. Oh, if only they knew.
NEW CO
COMIC
KILLER MAX
Mike Wade, the kind of film agent you only see in bad movies, is helping Hank option the film rights for Killer Max X. Mike says all the stuff you'd wanna hear.
I personally know Bruce Willis. We're like COUSINS. He owes me one.
Killer Max X will be a BLOCKBUSTER hit next summer!

I TOLD YOU WE'D BE HUGE, ETHAN!
All of this moderate success has gone to Hank's already swollen head.
So now, I'm wrapping up issue three. It's been a good distraction. Work is good for that. Otherwise-- all I can really seem to think about...
... is someone I let down.

CHELSEA, MANHATTAN
Aww, look at you and Booba there. You guys are best friends now.
All it takes is time. I ever tell you how long it took for Shugie to warm up to me? A whole SIX months. Before that, I could barely pet her.
UURRRRR
And now you two can run away together.
Well, we had a good run here, Gwen -- but the heart wants what the heart wants. You still have Booba here to keep you warm at night.

But if you're gone, what would I do without my little Buddha Belly? POKE POKE.
HEY, STOP THAT!
...I HATE getting older. Turning twenty-five sucks balls.
Your golden era of coconut ice cream binges are OVER. Calories actually catch up to you now.
You can't be a skinny Asian kid forever.
YES, I CAN! I'll weigh 147 lbs. until the day I die!
I'll have it carved on your tombstone. Now QUIET, I'm narrowing down the peeps for your birthday party next week.
We should've just had a joint party since our birthdays are so close together.
That's dumb. Let's see... Mark can make it. His wife will stay home with the kid.
He should just bring the kid to the bar. I'm sure we can get some apple juice for her.

Brian's back from Paris. Have you talked to him yet?
Tomorrow night.

I'll invite him and Ash myself.
Ugh... ASH? Do you HAVE to?

I don't want him hitting on my friends -- especially since I know most of 'em would actually sleep with him.

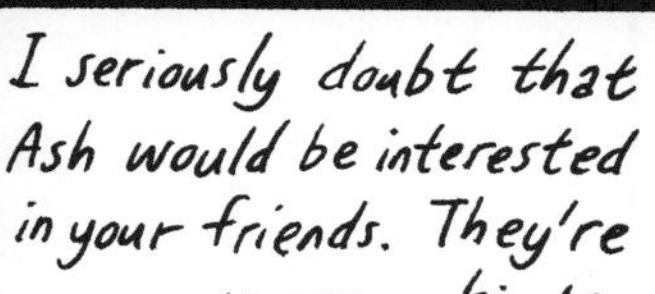
I seriously doubt that Ash would be interested in your friends. They're kinda--

KINDA **WHAT?**

Kinda... NOT as adorable as you.
Good save.

Oh - ahem - I also invited April.

WHAT?!

I always liked her.

Jesus, Gwen! Why don't you just invite my brother?! Or Sin!

How COULD I? You've never introduced me to EITHER!

And with DAMN GOOD reason, sweetie!

Correct me if I'm wrong, but didn't you patch things up with Patrick already?

We were BEHAVED when Dad was in the hospital. That's different.

I just don't get why you've come to HATE certain people so much.

-sigh- It's not HATE, Gwen. It's not that simple ...

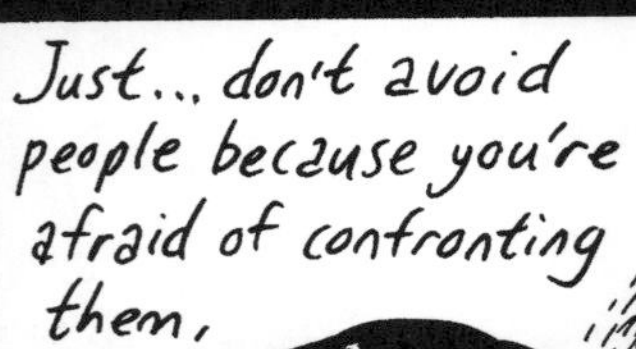

Just... don't avoid people because you're afraid of confronting them, Ethan.

THANKS, MOM.

HAWK
Damn, I totally feel for that wallflower over there...
BUZZCOCKS
EXI
What -- THAT guy?
Yeah, yeah, him.
The guy just looks lost. One of us should head on over and flirt with him.
You can casually walk up and say something like, "Hey, man, nice penis."
I can't imagine a single person -- gay or straight -- saying that.

You might be wondering why the guys and I are hanging out at THE HAWK, NYC's manliest gay bar. Well, remember that gay erotica gig I had a while back? Yes? No? Anyhoozers, the writer FINALLY got around to publishing it, and here we are at the release party. A Guys' Night Out for the ages...
...but then these MOFOS have to go and spoil it.
So, yeah... April. This feud you still have with her. Have you moved on yet?
So is THIS the intervention?
Ash caught me up to speed. From what I hear -- I think you're projecting your anger with Patrick onto April.
Okay, Brian, you can put the psychiatrist hat away. You're back in the states two minutes and you're already analyzing me.
But he DOES have a point, don't you think?
No! No point. Listen -- we ALL have issues with our family. We ALL harbor resentment. Don't single ME out like it's some rare EFFIN' brain disorder.

Brian, you BARELY speak to your passive-aggressive mom anymore.
Yeah, throw that back in my face now...
Ash, YOU haven't even seen your sister in five years. FIVE YEARS, MAN!
She's an asshole...
Exactly, see? Just lemme deal with Patrick -- AND APRIL -- my own way. I'm a big boy. I wipe my own butthole and everything.
Okay, you've had a bit too much to drink.
It's empty anyway.
Just trying to help out, man.
Well, maybe next time we'll have that big breakthrough I have coming. Right, Dr. Brian?
Grow up.
Hey, man, nice penis!
Right back at ya!
Ten points for irony. That was pretty fuckin' funny.
How come I didn't get hit on?

"KANE PACKER: MAN OF MEN."
Pulitzer material right there.
"...and Kane stared seductively at the young stud acrass the bar. His rippling arms glistened under perfect lighting, his juicy lips waiting to be kissed. Kane walked over in full confidence, packing junk as thick as a baby's forearm."
BABY'S FOREARM? EW...
Pretty amazing euphemism, huh, Shugie?

ETHAN...
ETHAN!
GIVE ME YOUR HAND! PLEASE!
ETHAN!!

NEW YORK SUPER DUPER CON

NYSDC SPRING 201

KILLER MAX

Hey, girl. Want to check out a GREAT new comic?

Um... no, thanks.

This is Hank's first comic convention. I'm not sure what he was expecting to happen, but I'm going to take a wild guess and say that Hank is not used to rejection (especially from geeks). You can practically see his massive ego deflating as we speak.

Oh, Becky, I think that's the comic that Roger was talking all about. Wanna check it out?
No, why waste your cash? Let's hit the toy booths.
I gotta stretch these legs a bit, Hank.
Okay, but don't be gone for too long. The fans will be here soon--I can FEEL it.
Sure.
YOU HAVE ONE MESSAGE:
"Hi, son, it's your mother. I'm calling to see if you are available for a birthday dinner. Call me back."
-BEEP-

I wonder where Gwen is right now. Haven't seen or heard from her all day.
NYSDC
WAR
Hello, Ethan, how are you?
Wait... SHIT... I KNOW THAT FUCKIN' VOICE...
JORDAN!
Long time no see.

I saw your new comic. Killer... Sam... Z...?
Haven't grown out of that superhero stage yet?
Nope, guess not...
Man, I envy you, Ethan. You get to relax and work on something... what's the word I'm looking for? SOPHOMORIC.
My agent, he's been putting SO much pressure on me to finish my next book. With comics as AVANT GARDE as mine, you can't just RUSH it, you know?
Count your lucky stars, my friend. You've got no IDEA what it's like to have your art held to such HIGH STANDARDS.
Yeah, heh, lucky me.
Once--just ONCE--I wish it were legal to punch another human being right in the fuckin' face. RIGHT IN HIS SMUG LITTLE FACE...
HOLY SHIIIIIIT. That is one SICK costume.
600
OUT OF MY WAY.

GOOD AFTERNOON, ETHAN...

Alone at last.
his can't be happening this
ppening this can't be happ
can't be happening this ca
be happening this can't be
ing this can't be happenin
this can't be happening this
be happening this can't be
this can't be happen
This can't be happening.

OH, BUT IT IS!
PUNCH!

Wakey, wakey, Ethan...
AHH!!
UH-UH. I'd calm down if I were you...
Wher-- OW--where are we?
An abandoned factory in Flatbush. Not too far from where you live.

Where I LIVE?! How the FUCK is it even possible for the NAZI SWINE to BE here?! It's that HOBO'S fault, I KNOW it!
You must be wonderin' why I'm even HERE, huh?
"This all started after your buddies came to rescue you. Me and Ratso was fightin' it out with the bunny, when all of a sudden I'm hit with this big flash of light."
"Next thing I know, I wake up in some strange land, covered in snow. I was pretty confused. No clue where I was. Not until I saw..."
"...YOU. You walking with ANOTHER hairless ape. I put two and two together-- I was in YOUR world."

"My first thought was to run over and BASH your brains into the damn ground."
"I wanted to -- BADLY-- but then I remembered..."
"...there was that time you beat me with ONE PUNCH--then threw my butt in jail. Whenever I think of that... my blood just BOILS. So, I had to wonder to myself..."
"...were you that SUPERHERO who kicked my ass? Or the mere mortal who I tossed into the dungeon like an old rag doll? No way to tell--so I waited. I followed you, watched you, and waited..."
"I drifted for weeks, unsure of what my next move would be. I didn't know how many of you hairless apes had powers, and I didn't want to be seen, so I had to avoid EVERYONE. I got around through alleyways, tunnels, and rooftops. I would run into a vagrant sometimes -- they were always too damn drunk to care. Then one night..."
Hey. HEY! That a... is that a fuckin' SWASTIKA on yer head?!

No trouble here, sir...
My daddy DIED in WW2! Come here so I can smack th--
RGH!!
CRACK
"I couldn't believe it at first. I crushed that bum's arm like I was squeezing just a rotten BANANA. Back in MY world, I was just a second-rate thug. But HERE... I could be a FREAKIN' GOD!"
"To make sure it wasn't just no fluke, I tested my newfound SUPERSTRENGTH on every bum and hobo I could find. Each snapped limb gave me a rush. I even crushed a stray cat with nothin' but my THUMB. Funny how your animals don't talk... but they all SCREAM the same! HAHA!"

Had an EPIPHANY, too, of all things. I realized that YOU--Ethan--are a NOBODY. Just like everyone else in this world...
...YOU ARE WEAK, YOU ARE SLOW, AND YOU ARE VERY BREAKABLE.
Yet SOMEHOW--you found your way into MY world and once made a FOOL outta me.
You get why that just PISSES me off, yeah? You get why I got to KILL YA, yeah?
Galen wouldn't let me OFF you and the rabbit that night in the dungeon. He always felt killing should be more... poetic. I'll take his advice for once.
Tonight, you will meet me on the Brooklyn Bridge. At midnight, to be exact.
That will be the time and place of your death. Poetic, eh?

Th--That's LUDICROUS, man. I... I don't want to fight you...

Oh, did I mention that I've kidnapped your little Gwen?

You--YOU MOTHERFUC--

-TSK TSK- Do you kiss your mother with that mouth, Ethan? If you upset me, I might not let Gwen live long enough to see me **CRUSH YOUR JAW.**

And I wouldn't bother calling the authorities, either. A knife can't even scratch my skin. I doubt an ARMY could even stop me right now.
Just you and me, Ethan...

And OHH, the joy I'll have when I snap your tiny neck in front of your fat little girlfriend's eyes. I'll drink her tears for dessert.
And then I'll conquer this world.

TA TA, Hero! See you tonight...

I... I finally know the true meaning of KAFKAESQUE...

Later that day...
Ethan?
That should be enough food for a week.
CAT FOOD
ETHAN?! What the fuck are you doing?! That's enough chow to last until the fuckin' RAPTURE!
You left me that really ODD message...

Yeah, sorry about that.
I tried calling Sin first, but she didn't answer. Sorry...
SHIT! Did you get hit with a hammer or something?
A pig, actually.
A PIG?
Listen, April...
I need you to take care of the cats for me. I've purchased enough food to last for a whole two months.
Wait-- WHAT?!
Take this, it's a money order for $3,627. That's ALL of my savings. Plus-- there's a letter for my mom in case I don't return.
You had THAT much in your savings account?
I have NO WAY to explain what's really happening to me right now. If I told you everything that's happened, you'd think I was making it all up.

You're one of the few people I'd trust to look after them, April.
Goodbye, Shugie.
Thanks, April. BYE!
BYE...

Brooklyn Bridge, 11:57 p.m.

Are they filming some sort of movie here?

Tsk tsk. The hero of the hour is nowhere to be seen. Figured he CARED more. What an AWFUL boyfriend.

Please don't take this personal, dear. It's just revenge.
-muffled speech-

STEP AWAY FROM MY WOMAN, SWINE!

Heh, you really cut it close there, Ethan. BRAVE MAN...
Listen, Swine...
I MAY BE A LIBERAL VEGAN PACIFIST--BUT I'M GONNA KICK YER
FAT NAZI PIG ass
FROM HERE TO QUEENS!!
HOLY SHIT, IS THAT JET LI?
NAH, IT'S JACKIE.
WITH A HAMMER?! HA! THANKS, I COULD USE A NICE MASSAGE!

There's one thing I need to know, Swine.
You said you got transported here while you and Ratso were fighting Faye...
Yeah, what of it?
I was transported here in the same WHITE FLASH as you, and it was WAY after your fight with Faye.
WHAT?!
Yet... I SAW Ratso's body and you were NOWHERE to be found...
I don't like what I'm hearing, Ethan. I'll give you a chance to take back what you just said. It'll make your DEATH a little less agonizing. GOT IT?
SWINE... YOU'RE NOTHING BUT A BIG, FAT, LOUSY COWARD! GOT IT?!

MUST
REALLY
WANNA
DIE
Look at that wire-work!
PEPPER

GAH!!
EAT THIS, A-HOLE!
WHAM BAM THANK YOU MA'AM
CRAP...

ARGH!!
WOW, that sounded REAL!
Miss-- are you okay?
-muffled speech-

OW! OW! OW! PAIN! ARM! PAIN! SHIT!
All these idiots cheer for you like you're some dumb movie star.
You really thought you could TAKE ME IN A FIGHT?!
BOY...
...ALL YOU'VE DONE IS MAKE ME REALLY, REALLY...

OH GOD OH
GOD OH GOD OH
OH GOD OH GOD OH
GOD OH GOD OH GOD
OH GOD OH GOD OH
GOD OH GOD OH GOD OH
OH GOD OH GOD OH
GOD OH GOD OH
OH GOD OH

SMASH!

Ethan!
It's about time you woke up. How are you feeling?
Crusader...? Oh god, please don't tell me it's been another ten years...
Ten years?
A-After the explosion, I went back to my world again.
Ethan, you've been with ME the whole time after the explosion--which was only moments ago.
I can't be sure, but I think...

...this is the AFTERLIFE.

I'm... DEAD.
There is SO MUCH stuff going through my mind right now... SO MUCH STUFF.
How long have I really been dead? Did that whole confrontation with Swine even happen--or was it just some dream?
Is Crusader wrong and this is just another time slip? If... if I'm TRULY dead...
...I'm never gonna have sex again, watch TV again, pet a cat, eat pasta, or even take a shit again...
((can you take a shit in the AFTERLIFE?)
It took a little while for everything to sink in--I mean--to REALLY sink in.
There was only one way to cope...

Well, that's ONE question answered: you can definitely CRY here in the AFTERLIFE.
I just cried and cried for... I dunno... HOURS? EONS? Who knows?
SOB
-ahem-
Any day now...
Oh no...
SWINE?

Look at what I found...
Ethan--you want to stop CRYING for one moment to notice this?
WHO CARES?! -SOB- I'M DEAD!!
And you can sure get a whole lot DEADER! NOW MOVE!

WHAT'S HE DOING IN MY AFTERLIFE?!
OUR AFTERLIFE! AND YOU THINK WE CAN FLY HERE?!
AHHHHHHH
GUESS WE CAN.
YOU THINK I CAN'T--?

OW.
That's the... oddest thing I've EVER seen. Dead OR alive.
That was... me.
That was YOUR giant hand?
I imagined a giant hand swatting Swine away--and then THAT happened.
Hmm... giant hand...
Not exactly my weapon of choice--but we'll stick with what works for now.

You think this might be HELL, Crusader?
For you? Dunno.
For us cats, Hell is full of fleas and loud, sudden noises. Heaven is full of tuna and catnip.
Swine is here. He's after us-- after ME. When the villain's around, it can't be Heaven.
Or maybe it's just a projection, like that giant hand.
Yeah, maybe...
But then YOU could be a projection, also.
Or vice versa.
Hmm...
Looks like we're gonna be best DEAD friends.
That's, um, not really very funny, Ethan.
Sorry. I use humor to lighten the situation. Why aren't you freaking out more? You're pretty level.

I've been at death's door before. You could say I've been prepared. Honestly, I thought we shoulda been goners after our van got ambushed.
And you mentioned some PUG.
Oh, jeez, I'd almost forgotten about that.
Pug?
That's the last thing we talked about, you remember? "All for a stupid pug." Those were your words. Care to elaborate?
I mean, we got LOTS of time.
I was just thinking out loud that time. It's really nothing...
The pug wasn't really the problem.
For the record, I used to defend you ALL the time. The others... let's just say they weren't your biggest fans.
Defending you wasn't the most POPULAR opinion.
Yeah, but now you've definitely realized how all of this is MY fault, right? First-- I ruined your world. Now-- we're dead.
Yes, I think you're an awful OMEN OF DEATH, Ethan.
Heh. Thanks.
Let me ask you...
...now that you're DEAD, what regrets do you have?

Too many to count, Crusader. You?
Not saving the world. That would be the big one on my list.
Well... that pretty much trumps anything on MY list.
I have smaller regrets, too. Like never fixing my relationship with my older brother.
That's been on my mind recently.
You had a brother?
Yup, we were both superpowered. Only I was more... gifted.
More powerful.
I flew faster, jumped higher. I could punch a whole mountain.
We inherited our gifts from our father--who FORBADE us to become crime fighters, you believe that?
Our dad commanded us to BLEND into society. HIDE our talents.
"Go get some REAL WORK," he would say.
He told us to stop dreaming of grander things. Heh... boy, were we defiant.
Dad was a major PRICK then.
Yeah... I know what you mean...

Whoa... this is certainly strange. Are you crying on the inside?
Not exactly, no. Maybe it just rains here.
I wouldn't count on a 'maybe' here.
Well... I'm stumped.

Crusader... why aren't you blinking?
YOU THOUGHT YOU COULD ESCAPE FROM ME?!!
OH.
Yeah. OH.
YOU AND I HAVE SOME UNFINISHED BUSINESS!

CRAP!!
We need us some GIANT HAND-SLAPPING POWER, Ethan! ANY DAY NOW!!
I'M THINKING IT, BUT IT AIN'T HAPPENING!
I've given more to this world than you could FATHOM with that peanut-sized brain.
Wait a minute-- this speech...

...it's the speech I wrote for Galen. Am I just gonna keep running into ALL of my awful creations now?!
Yet my legacy is but a footnote in history--unlike YOU!
But what's with his face? It looks like...
...my father?
YOU with your grandstanding heroics-- your GIFTS!
OKAY--prosaic metaphors aside, I think I may end up pooping my pants.
GIFTS you never had to EARN!

SHUT UP!

That seemed to work.
Lucky us. Any single idea what this was meant to be?
Nah...
let's go... before something else gets thrown at us. I need to wish myself a new pair of pants.
New pants?
Long story.

Are you religious, Crusader?
Not until GOD shows up here. YOU?
Not really... but I always hoped that death would lead to a higher state of self-consciousness. Super ZEN stuff.
Like, maybe we'd start seeing the universe in twelve dimensions. But instead, all I'm dwelling on are the small, PETTY things in life. It's really a letdown.
I don't think so, though. I mean... some petty things can actually be the biggest things in our world. That's why we can't get past them.
Now we have a whole eternity to try.
Heh--we had to die before we could get therapy.

Yeah, could've used some a lot sooner. Especially after my brother and I became REAL superheroes.

We were both rookies for the Mighty Union, the most prestigious superteam on the planet. It was great at first-- to be around others like us.

Then--I quit. The Union wasn't for me. We barely ever did any REAL superhero stuff. It was all politics.

My brother was FURIOUS. In his mind, succeeding with the Mighty Union was the only way to prove our father wrong. But not for me. I had my OWN plans. My OWN destiny.

But you showed them--becoming the greatest hero of Catropolis.
Yeah, until YOU showed up. Heh.
-sigh- But some hero I turned out to be, right? I eventually let Catropolis down.
Yeah, but real heroes never QUIT--and you never did.
Eh, you can stop with the platitudes. You sound like my ex-wife.
Wait--you were MARRIED?
Yeah...? AND?
Uh... sorry. I didn't mean to offend you. I just never pictured you having a wife. It's... cute.

!
YES, IT'S DEFINITELY CUTE, ETHAN.
Come join us, Crusader.
YOU SHOULDN'T BE HERE! I'VE HAD-- CLOSURE! I'VE PUT YOU BEHIND ME, DAMNIT!
Such a broken record, Ethan. You know I'll always be with you -- even in the AFTERLIFE.

GREAT, NOW YOUR SISTER IS HERE, TOO?! LEAVE US ALONE, YOU DAMN WITCH!
Oh my, Crusader doesn't know, does he? Now--THIS is interesting. You've been lying to him this whole time?
So is she, like, your cousin?
No, Crusader, I'm his EX. From HIS world--where YOU'RE originally from. Where little Ethan CREATED you.
THAT'S LUDICROUS! ETHAN, YOU'VE GOT SOME CRAZY FAMILY MEMBERS!!

Crusader, why do you think Ethan was more powerful than any other being? HE CREATED YOU ALL--LIKE A GOD! ONLY HE'S A LOSER!
"Search your feelings, Crusader. You KNOW IT to be true!" HAHAHAHA! God, look at your STUPID FACE!
Systematically lying to your own CARTOON. That's a new low, Ethan...
Grrr...
SNAP
We--We've done this dance before. It's getting really OLD...
I don't do this to be CRUEL, Ethan. There is METHOD to my MADNESS. Why do you think I'm still around? Could it have something to do with all that lingering GUILT?

I've already said my sorries. Sorry I was such a DICK to you--is that ENOUGH?!
Everybody loves a good martyr. But let's dig deeper. There's something larger that's at the pit of your stomach...
...the fact that you never really loved me.
W-What? That's not true.
Sure, Ethan...

I'VE ONLY MET YOU TWICE AND I ALREADY LOATHE YOU!
We... should talk.

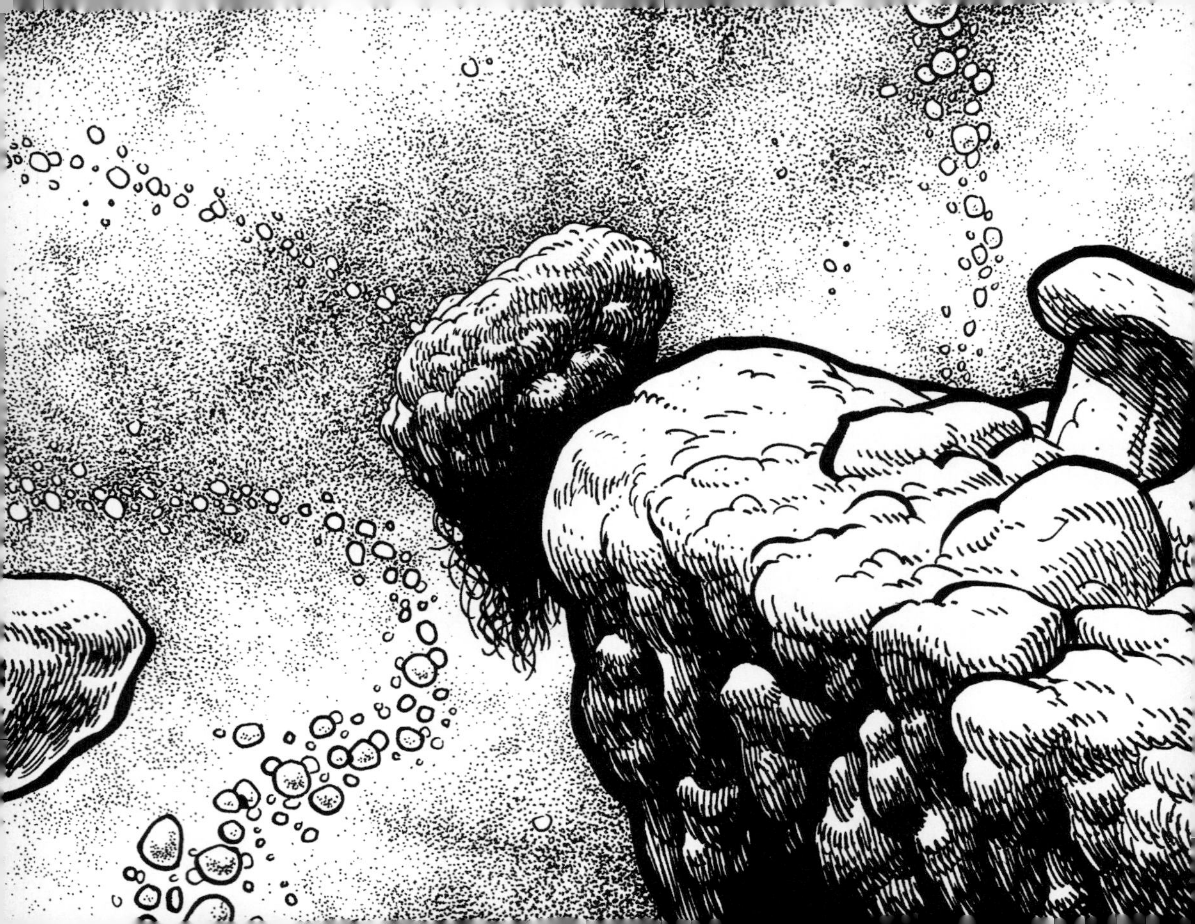

Awkward moments also occur here, in case you were keeping a tally.
I went through everything with Crusader. I owed him that much. (OWE him?)

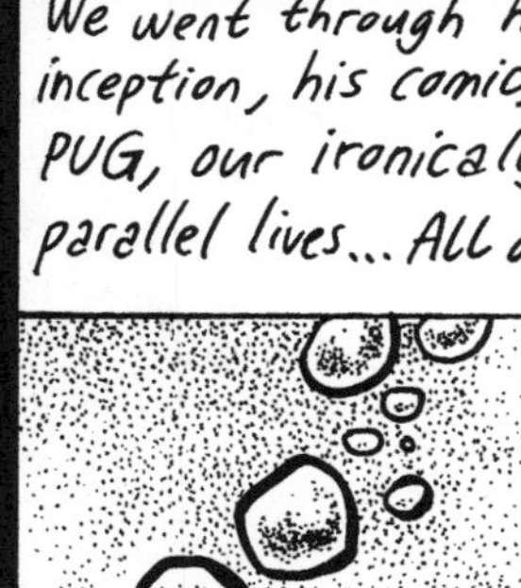

We went through his inception, his comic, the PUG, our ironically parallel lives... All of it.

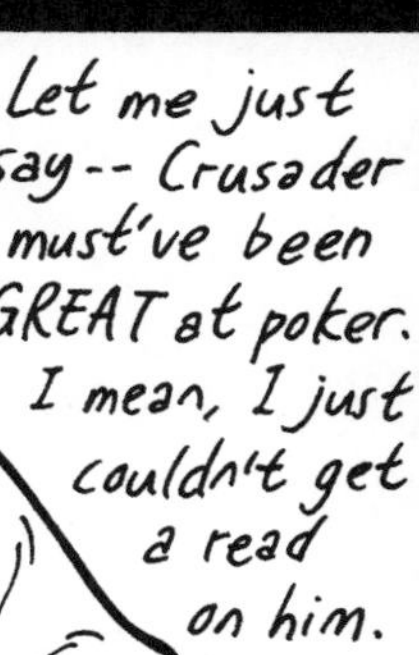

Let me just say-- Crusader must've been GREAT at poker. I mean, I just couldn't get a read on him.

Was he sad to learn that his entire life was all make-believe? Or was he planning to beat me into a massive coma with my own left arm? (Not that that matters here, being DEAD and all...)

All of this made Crusader's response ... surprising.

So...you never loved Sin? Is that TRUE?

Huh.

Um...no, actually. I did love her. She was my FIRST love, in fact.

But...you were never IN love, right? I'm only taking an educated guess here.

-sigh- I really, really wanted to be. I think I even convinced myself for a time. THAT didn't last...
I know. Same here. With my ex-wife, I mean. We went on a first date that never ended.
I was just thinking that.
YUP.
When somebody is such a big part of your life, it's hard to really see the faults, and even harder to FACE them.
And even though you see the end coming, it still destroys you inside.
And then you'd do ANYTHING to win them back. I know I did.
And if THAT doesn't work, you make them the villain... which can backfire... badly.
Then the GUILT comes.
By the way, we should really be doing this with beers.
YOU DRINK?

So I imagined us a couple of beers. Then a couple more. Then a whole bunch. We couldn't manage to get ourselves drunk, but just the taste of cold beers brought a little sense of normalcy back...
It's the shared struggle, Ethan. That's the glue that holds together an imperfect union.
For us--it was fostering cats.
That still blows my mind.
That there are CATS in my world?
How would you feel if there was a different version of YOU in some other reality?
Point taken.
What were your cats' names?
Sin had Clarkie, Petey, Lana, LiL'Bub, and Bram.
ME--I had Honey, Chewie, Tobey, Othello, Murdock, and...
...SHUGIE.

That's Shugie? That's what cats look like in your world?
Yes.
That's crazy. No clothes?
Shugie?
I think that's universal for 'FOLLOW ME.'
Right...
This could be another DEATH OMEN for all we know.
Okay, ignore me...

Whoa.
I'm guessing this means more to you than me.
It's my childhood home--when my family and I lived in that tiny apartment in Chinatown.
It's like some twisted dream, but I can almost... feel it.

We haven't had a good track record here.
You can stay out here if you'd like.
It's not like we're joined at the--
--hip.
Is this what you were expecting?
Yes...
...but that doesn't make it any less jarring.

That's you and Patrick, I can assume?
YUP.
You look a lot like him.
We used to draw at that old table for hours.
Usually before our dad got home, or during long weekends. Hours at this old table.
I first learned how to draw by watching him and copying him.
After a while though, he became more of a coach than a brother.
Your best friend--and your worst enemy all in one.
Crusader...
...what ever happened to your brother?

After our falling out? Nothing good. He was kicked out of the Union, and eventually fell into villainy. He joined the Mutant Rogues.
Years and years of experimentation and gene splicing -- it changed him. HORRIBLY.
When I saw him again... it broke my heart.
He's not even a cat anymore, is he?
Oh, sure I am...
MEOW.

That's funny, brother. You're sick.
By the way, I don't appreciate being slapped by a giant hand. Let me return the FAVOR.
ETHAN!
OW.
OW.
OW.

YOU SICK BASTARD!
Oh, calm down, you SPOILED SNOT!
It's not like he's gonna DIE! HA!
W-Who the HELL are you calling spoiled? I'm SPOILED now?!
SPOILED ROTTEN! I was Dad's PUNCHING BAG growin' up. I looked after your sorry ass before I was just kicked aside. Now where is my RESPECT, huh?!
God, how did the T-800 do this again?
I can see that your ENVY has led you to develop DELUSIONS OF GRANDEUR.

Dad kicked ME around as well!! You want to keep playing the SAD LITTLE ABUSED BOY? Would you like a MEDAL for it?! How 'bout a plate of fresh cookies?!
I took care of you, YA USELESS PILE OF FUR! We coulda been the TWO GREATEST HEROES IN HISTORY! But NO--you thought you were BETTER than me, right? You thought you knew more about the world, yeah?!
QUIT REWRITING HISTORY, YOU SELF-RIGHTEOUS PRICK! I was your ONLY friend--you remember THAT?! You needed to mentor more than I needed to BE mentored. And THAT is why you couldn't handle the fact that I pursued my OWN PATH--leaving YOU behind! This all leads back to your bruised ego, SWINE!
I didn't want you throwing your LIFE away! I knew what was BEST for ya! I was looking out for YOU! ALL I've ever done as a big brother was try to HELP you. YOU! You SPOILED BRAT!
HELP?!! I DIDN'T NEED YOUR HELP! I was an ADULT, and you were trying to control me, the way you try to CONTROL EVERYTHING! It wasn't ALTRUISM on your part--it was just PLAIN ARROGANCE!

DEEP DOWN INSIDE--YOU'RE STILL JUST THE SAME SAD COWARD WHO COULDN'T STAND UP TO OUR FATHER!
FINE... I'M A COWARD. AND YOU KNOW WHAT? YOU'RE JUST LIKE ME.
I WILL NEVER BE LIKE YOU!
EVER

I'VE WORKED HARD-- HARD TO BECOME THE CAT I AM!
YOU HEAR ME, PIG?!
THIS IS MY LIFE! DAD COULDN'T CONTROL ME--
--AND YOU COULDN'T CONTROL ME! NOBODY CAN!!

Maybe this IS Hell...
Oh, far from it, Ethan.
VERY far...
FRANK.
You remembered. How flattering.
One moment, please.

There, that's better. Had to get outta that dark cave setting. Too icky.
Long time no see, Ethan.
Hope this little adventure hasn't been TOO taxing on you both.
You stupid son of a BITCH! This is all YOUR fault! This posthumous therapy group hug is just another sick, twisted GAME of yours! Is this how you get your rocks off, JERKFACE?!
Well, CLEARLY Ethan isn't gonna be reasonable today. How 'bout YOU, Crusader? Been a while for us as well.
WAIT! YOU KNEW HIM? HOW DID THIS NOT COME UP?!!
Hey, YOU never mentioned a MAGIC HOBO either--don't look at ME! Besides, he's a damn RACCOON in my world.

Howdy!
STOP IT, FRANK.
Is this punishment because we didn't want to play your stupid game?
PUNISHMENT? That's harsh. This is more like enlightenment if you ask me.
God, I wanna PUNCH you. We're DEAD 'cause of YOU.
This place is more like a waiting room--you're not dead. In reality, you're still fighting SWINE.
(And yeah, I'll admit, I had a small hand in that.)
And YOU, Crusader, you're still in Galen's lair. Unconscious and half-dead, but you're technically still alive.
So I'm gonna take a WILD guess here...
... either we play your game and make one of your 'choices'-- or we head into the light, right?
Now you're starting to sound like Ethan. LOOK-- I'm not CRUEL. You can return to your normal lives...
... EXCEPT ... only ONE of you gets to go back. THAT is the deal.
You... SCUM.

Scum? I'm hurt. This is a PERFECTLY fair deal. I'm being generous and--if I do say so myself--quite benevolent here. I could just send you BOTH into the REAL afterlife.
Oh, and trust me, you DON'T want that.
Frank, why can't you just send us BOTH back? You're practically a GOD. I think. We're at your mercy here. YOU know it and WE know it. Why are you still playing these GAMES with us? You're just picking on a boy and his cartoon. What's the POINT to all of this?!!
First, I'm flattered that you think I might be a GOD. I'm not. Second, there IS a point to all of this, Crusader--and I think you know what it is.
You both keep calling this 'my game,' whereas I call this a LESSON.
LESSON??!!

You really ARE just --JUST TWISTED! We've been through ALL this crap simply for YOUR entertainment! I ca--YOU KNOW WHAT?! I'M JUST GONNA REARRANGE YOUR FACE AND MAKE YOU EAT YOUR OWN TESTICLES!!
Offer is limited time only, tough guy.
Ethan...
Come on, Crusader, this BITCH can't take the BOTH of us!
Ethan... I'll do it. Okay? I'll die so that you can live.
WHAT?! NO! Listen--BUDDY--now is NOT the time to be making any courageous sacrifices.
It's not that, Ethan.
Then WHAT?
I've already lost everything important to me.
No, don't you see? I can CHANGE all of it. I'm still your creator!
Then that's no different than letting FRANK control my life. I'm tired of being a puppet.
Agreeing to this makes you EXACTLY that!
NO--because this way I'LL be deciding my own fate. Ethan, no matter how you slice it, I'm still a cartoon. I'm still a drawing on some sheet of paper with all of YOUR baggage!

It's time to let go.
This is insane! INSANE!! I'm arguing with my own CARTOON! This is like a bad acid trip! Not to mention THIS bozo!
Ethan-- let ME be the hero today. You go back and live your life. Try to make peace.
Crusader... if it were THAT easy to make peace with everyone, I probably wouldn't even BE here.
I meant make peace with YOURSELF, Ethan.
Time's up.
Goodbye, Ethan...

...I'll see you
in another life.

GET OFFA ME!
I GOT MY RIGHTS!
?
I GOT RIGHTS!!
Baby-- are you OKAY?!
G-GWEN? GWEN! What's--? I--
That crazy fucker dressed like a PIG just started HITTING attendees.

He just walked straight up to Jordan and CLOCKED him across his face COLD.
I'm just glad that security showed up before he messed with that adorable mug.
Heh.
Uh oh.
You got that look on your face that worries me.
I missed you.
Oh... Yeah, I missed you, too. Lighten up.

GLASS COMICS PRESENTS KILLER MAX X in...
PERTINENT EON
PART 3
HANK GLASS
writer · creator · creative director
ETHAN YOUNG · art
HANK GLASS
editor · editor in chief · publisher
KILL-O-METER

You really could've made the monster POP a bit more, Ethan.
If the art were better, we'd be selling more copies. That's probably the reason our sales have declined month to month.
Hank, that's actually NOT uncommon for single issues. That's the way the market works for most comics, in fact.
You should've put more EMOTIONAL CONTENT into this page.
Gee, Hank, maybe YOU should've written a story that read higher than a 4th grade level!
Excuse me?
YOUR. WRITING. BLOWS. CHUNKS.
"Annnnnnnd THAT'S how I was let go."

Can't you still finish the book, son? Not good to leave money behind.
I'll land on my feet.
Besides, this one particular gig was--How should I put this?--sucking the living SOUL outta me.
Why don't you do a book with Patrick? Think about how GOOD it will be!
-SIGH- You never know when to give up, do you, Mom?
Your brother wishes you a happy birthday. He said he was disappointed we couldn't all get together as a family.
Is that what he SAID, or is that what you're just gathering?

Son, listen to me. Those big fights you've had with Patrick won't look so big in the future.
Mom, I KNOW that. It's not like I'm unaware of that. It's not like I don't still love my older brother.
Believe it or not, I don't WANT to hold a grudge. But... 'moving on' is easier said than done. It wasn't just the HUGE fights we used to have -- it's everything. He was once my best friend... and my worst enemy. All in one. That about sums it up.
I know that all this shit, pardon my French, will seem silly in the future. But right now -- right THIS second -- Patrick and I are what we are. Sorry.
Well, if you won't let us celebrate your birthday as a family, let me give you your birthday money now. That drawer there.
-SIGH- You word everything JUST RIGHT, Mom.

I'm getting a bit too old to be taking cash from you now. God, you've got a lot of crap in here.
This can't be...
Do you remember that drawing?
I've held onto a small handful of your art for many years. I keep some in my desk, but I have a few more stored away in the closet. You were so talented at such a young age.

I wouldn't call this one of my finer pieces, though.
It feels like I just did this drawing yesterday. It's not easy to forget that night. I always wondered where some of my old doodles went. It shouldn't surprise me, really-- my mom being the way she is.
Mom tends to glorify her best memories, while pushing her worst ones behind a giant wall of denial. I love her, but she's very green at times.
Her greatest wish is to have a perfect family. Like in sitcoms. The kind of family that hugs and laughs and there's no such thing as resentment...
You look almost sad, son.
Are you okay?
...and sometimes...
I'm okay, Mom.
...I wish my mom and I could agree more on the idea of family.

I know I'm being really stubborn. I'll be the first one to admit it.
But let me say ONE thing in my defense:
Baby steps.
SOY
Hey. You cut your hair.
Well, I was tired of being mistaken for an ugly chick.

Ha. You look so young with this haircut. You're gonna get carded until your face is covered in wrinkles.

I hope not. But I AM looking forward to having gray hair. I think I'd look cool with that.

Hey, by the way, before I forget-- I've got a little gift for you. Sort of.
Sort of?! Uh oh.

I'm not gonna get a banana pie in the face, am I?

OH, HEY! Shugie's old favorite. You've had the toy this whole time!

Yeah, my kids are more into crumpled paper. I figured Shugie would want her 'mouse' back.

Your kids doin' okay?
They're all good. Yours?
Same. Nothing world-shattering. Chewie has gotten a bit chubbier. But all is good.
Good, good...
So... I have to ask. What made you finally decide to call again? Not that I wasn't glad to hear from you.
It just came out of nowhere.
Would you believe... it was Divine Intervention? Or is that too much of a stretch?
Considering how NOT religious you are? I'd say it's quite suspect. You haven't 'FOUND' religion like that one Baldwin, have you?
I've always described myself as more of an AGNOSTIC. Now-- I'm just confused. So, I don't have answers to either of your questions. Sorry.

So, I've become your default phone call whenever you suffer from a bout of EARLY LIFE CRISIS?
Hmm... I'm kind of torn between being honored and being WORRIED.
No need to be worried. I call you because... you know me better than anyone.
Even though we're not together anymore, it makes me feel at ease whenever we get to talk.
You know...you ever wonder what it'd be like if we stayed together?
Come on, Ethan, not THIS again.
Get over yourself. I'm not trying to get back together here.
Ha, fair enough. I think we're better off as friends.
Yeah, same here. Although staying together might have prevented some of my WACKIER existential breakdowns.

I don't know if I should ask for an explanation. But always remember-- Hemingway SHOT himself, and he was also a crazy cat lady. So that's PLUS ONE in your win column.
Jeez, you always know how to look on the bright side of things, don't you, Sin?
"The power of accurate observation..."
"...is commonly called CYNICISM by those who have not got it."
Heh... that's a great quote.
I know.

TO THE BIRTHDAY BOY!

May he remain 147 lbs. for all eternity. He'll die nice and slim.

I can't believe you told him, Gwen.

Serves you right for being so vain.

I'm not THAT vain.
By the way, where's April? I thought you invited her tonight.

You didn't want her to come, remember? So, I uninvited her. Besides, she said she was busy with other plans tonight.

Oh, okay...

HAPPY 25TH! *MUAH*
Okay, WAY too much whiskey for you.
A quarter-century old. I see really exciting things in your future.
Let's all drink to it!
And Mark was right-- there WERE exciting things around the bend.
A few months after my birthday, my publishing deal with Locusts Comics expired. I decided to reboot 'Crusader Pug' into a new 'Crusader CAT' comic. Only this time, I'm going to be SELF-publishing the series. I have all the artistic freedom in the world now. Scary...

I'm gonna try and build on the audience I've gained from Locusts. Hopefully, those same folks will respond positively to this 'reboot' of sorts. Crusader's got a whole lot of life left in him.
I don't expect to make a single DIME from this new comic (at least not for a few years). But truth be told, money is no longer my main driving force.
Not anymore...
I just want to FINALLY do my character some justice.

Let's hope I get it right this time.
Aw, my sweet Gavin.
Babe, could you STOP babying Gavin? You know he has LEGS and can WALK, right?!
But he's tired. LOOK at him.
Good Lord.
Nobody WUVS my Gavin the way I do.
PANT PANT PANT
"Here's something you might not have known..."

...when you see a cat with a clipped ear, it means they've been fixed. It's part of the Trap-Neuter-Release program. Shugie, my little runt, has it on her ear. You may have noticed that Crusader Cat has it on the cover. If you haven't, look again.
I did it as an homage to Shugie. Yes, I do admit that I play favorites.
It's wrong, I know. And I love ALL my cats. Tobey, Murdock, Honey, Chewie, Othello, all of 'em. Even my ex's cats, Petey, Lana, Bram, Clarkie, and Lil' Bub, I still love them to death.
But from the moment I saw her, I felt connected to Shugie. Maybe it's because she was so meek. I had to PROTECT her, you know? I said to myself, "I'm already fostering a ZILLION cats, what's one more?" Ha, I'm sure that's what EVERY hoarder has said at one point or another.
Shugie was a project. She was extremely skittish at first. You couldn't pet her for more than a second before she bolted. The fact that I was the one who originally trapped her as a stray probably didn't help. It took months and months of work. Then one night, while sleeping on my couch, Shugie started cuddling up next to my feet. Kinda out of nowhere.
As weeks passed, Shugie got braver and started sleeping closer and closer to my actual body. Eventually, she claimed the area beside my stomach as HER sleeping spot. Her purring became my default white noise.
Now, you might think that this whole story is a bit trivial, but here's why it matters...

... I wanted to quit art at one point. Something I had been doing since the age of three, something I had always been good at. But yeah, there was a time when I just wanted to GIVE UP on my dreams of being a cartoonist.
Every struggling artist has their "should I just give up?" moment. If you're a struggling artist and you think you'll never succumb to such a moment of weakness, then life has a few more HARSH lessons to teach you, my friend. Trust me.
So... when I was at my lowest, I found solace in a cat. A cat with a clipped ear and stinky breath. A cat that took over six months for me to EARN her trust. That's the key word: EARN. Getting Shugie to trust me felt like my first real accomplishment after quitting art school. Rejection letters don't keep you warm at night, but cats certainly do. I even started talking to Shugie as therapy. She never talked back, obviously. She would just yawn.
And that's when I made the decision to never give up on my dreams. As crazy as it sounds, I made a promise to my CAT. A promise that I would succeed one day. A promise that I'd have a place of my own with plenty of room for all the critters to stretch their legs.
I know, sounds like a promise that a four-year-old would make.
What can I say? I'm a crazy cat lady trapped in an Asian boy's body.
I joke around and say Shugie's my soulmate, but I'm kinda half-serious when I say it. She's been with me through multiple apartments, multiple girlfriends, multiple jobs, multiple EVERYTHING. We've been through thick and thin together. Partners in crime.

It was just nice... having someone to come home to who didn't nag you, who wasn't disappointed in you, who didn't treat you like crap or make you feel unwanted. I never had pets as a child, and was always skeptical of how emotionally attached you could truly become with an animal. Little did I know.

So, for all those reasons -- I'm dedicating this first volume of 'Crusader Cat' to Shugie. Well, I'm actually dedicating the book to ALL of my critters, but with a special nod to my little angel.

What you're holding in your hand right now -- it wouldn't have been possible without them. So... enjoy.

Okay, so what do you think, Shugie?

Think it's a good intro?

Goodnight, Shugie...

...and goodnight, everyone...

...sweet dreams.